THE WOMEN'S WAR

Borgo Press Books by ALEXANDRE DUMAS

THE WOMEN'S WAR

A PLAY IN FIVE ACTS

ALEXANDRE DUMAS

Translated and Adapted by Frank J. Morlock

THE BORGO PRESS

MMXII

THE WOMEN'S WAR

DEDICATION

To Conrad—

Yet another project that would never have seen
the light of day without your support.

CONTENTS

CAST OF CHARACTERS

Baron de Canolles

Duke d'Épernon

Duke de la Rochefoucauld

Richon

Cauvignac

Ravailly

Barrabas

Linet, advisor to the Princess de Condé

Pompey, squire to the Vicomtess de Cambes

Castorin, lackey to Monsieur de Canolles

Biscarros, cook

Cortanvaux, squire to the Duke d'Épernon

An Officer

A Ferryman

Ferguson

Frigotin

Carrotel

Tax Collector

The Vicomtess de Cambes

Nanon de Lartigues

The Princess de Condé

Dowager

Madame de Tourville

Francinette, Nanon's servant

An Executioner

Soldiers

Men and Women of the People

ACT I

SCENE 1

The Ferry of Ison. At the front, the road leading to the ferry. To the right a tree with nets drying on it, and a bench to the left, the Ferryman's cabin. Further back, the Dordogne River.

The Ferryman is sleeping in his cabin. Ferguson is up the tree.

FERGUSON

Nothing by land; nothing by sea. Forty degrees of heat and the grasshoppers are en masse. That's all. You can come, Captain.

CAUVIGNAC

(appearing)

Good!

(calling in a half voice)

You can come, Barrabas.

BARRABAS

Here I am!

CAUVIGNAC

Where is Carrotel?

BARRABAS

He found a fig tree and he's eating some figs.

CAUVIGNAC

Have you looked out the window?

BARRABAS

I looked.

CAUVIGNAC

What's the Ferryman doing?

BARRABAS

Sleeping.

CAUVIGNAC

Well, we are still short one man.

BARRABAS

Frigotin? He won't fail.

CAUVIGNAC

Where is he then?

BARRABAS

He's inspecting the fish shed; but he doesn't have a key.

CAUVIGNAC

Fine!

(goes into the cabana and shouts)

Hey!

BARRABAS

I have to have a talk with him. Hey, Mr. Ferryman.

FERRYMAN

(groaning)

Hum!

CAUVIGNAC

Come, come, a little good humor—some good humor for a shilling.

FERRYMAN

A shilling—the Devil!

CAUVIGNAC

Let's get a move on.

FERRYMAN

You want to cross the river, sir?

CAUVIGNAC

We are at the Ison Ferry, right?

(Barrabas goes into the cabana through the window and makes a search.)

FERRYMAN

Yes, sir.

CAUVIGNAC

And this little house in the trees, isn't it inhabited by a young lady of twenty or twenty-two?

FERRYMAN

Yes, exactly, and by a little chamber maid who has such eyes—

CAUVIGNAC

Do you know the lady's name?

FERRYMAN

No.

CAUVIGNAC

And the name of the servant?

FERRYMAN

Oh, that one, that's another matter. That's Mademoiselle Francinette.

CAUVIGNAC

That's it! Is the dock in good shape?

FERRYMAN

If you don't fish.

CAUVIGNAC

Ah! You fish? It seems to me you don't fish in your hut.

FERRYMAN

Damn—when it's too hot, I sleep.

CAUVIGNAC

Apropos of the heat, is one absolutely forced to cool off in the river when one is at the Ison Ferry and one is thirsty?

FERRYMAN

No—if you have a tongue, you ask for wine and if you have money.

CAUVIGNAC

Yes—you pay—go find a bottle—make it the best.

FERRYMAN

I am going.

(He goes to the cellar—Cauvignac follows him. Hardly has he gone in the cellar when Cauvignac locks the door and bolts it.)

CAUVIGNAC

There.

FERRYMAN

Well, what are you doing?

CAUVIGNAC

What Cardinal Mazarin does when he finds a treasure.

FERRYMAN

What does he do?

CAUVIGNAC

He locks it up.

FERRYMAN

But you promised me a shilling.

CAUVIGNAC

An honest man has only his word, and since that's all I have, you shall have it. Now, gentlemen, come forward in the order I call you, Lt. Barrabas.

BARRABAS

Present!

CAUVIGNAC

Ensign Ferguson.

FERGUSON

Present!

CAUVIGNAC

Sergeant Carrotel, Lance Corporal Frigotin.

CARROTEL and FRIGOTIN

Present!

CAUVIGNAC

Gentlemen, you are the cadre of a corps which does not yet exist, it's true, but which cannot fail to exist if you give me intelligence and unanimous help.

BARRABAS

We will, Captain.

CAUVIGNAC

Since our entry into the country, we have escorted the Royal Tax Collector, who raised contributions for His Majesty, and, who, having passed over this ferry this morning to get to Lebourn, must necessarily re-cross it tonight. Do not forget this detail.

BARRABAS

No, Captain.

CAUVIGNAC

Foreknowledge of an event can be favorable to our interests.

BARRABAS

In the return to the tax collector?

CAUVIGNAC

Yes! I thought it our military duty to occupy the ferry of Ison on the Dordogne, a position which commands the river.

BARRABAS

Very good!

CAUVIGNAC

Moreover, I am waiting on a high and mighty lord.

BARRABAS

A high and mighty lord? Ah!

CAUVIGNAC

With whom I have to settle some family business. Without doubt, he will bring an escort with him. I desire not to be disturbed during our conference. Watch the escort and at the first gesture I make, shoot from the hip.. Now—hats off, hide your arms. We are boatmen and fisherman at the ferry of Ison—and we are waiting.

BARRABAS

For the fish to die, right?

FERGUSON

Oh, for the game to pass, understood.

CAUVIGNAC

They are full of intelligence. By the way, a last recommendation, you see that little house?

BARRABAS

Down there among the trees?

CAUVIGNAC

Yes, it could be that in your wanderings, you might wish to enter there for one reason or another.

BARRABAS

Damn!

CAUVIGNAC

Well, I desire that you not enter. It is inhabited by someone in my family. And now, take the most innocent airs you can. I have spoken.

BARRABAS

I am going to fish with a line.

FERGUSON

I am going to mend the nets.

CARROTEL

I will return to my fig tree.

CAUVIGNAC

Ah, Devil! Already someone is coming to us.

BARRABAS

Game or fish?

CAUVIGNAC

Game!

BARRABAS

(looking)

Oh! Oh! There's some kinds of game that eat the huntsmen.

FERGUSON

Bah! The tax collector. They're to be swallowed, they're sweet like honey.

TAX COLLECTOR

(entering)

Ferryman—hey.

CAUVIGNAC

Here, sir.

TAX COLLECTOR

Are you the Ferryman of Ison?

CAUVIGNAC

Yes, I am.

TAX COLLECTOR

Come on! You are Ramoneau—Ramoneau who ferries me all the time?

CAUVIGNAC

I didn't say I am Ramoneau, I told you I am the Ferryman.

TAX COLLECTOR

Yeah! What does that mean? Oh, I had those five brave partisans who gave me such a good escort on my way—tell me, my friend, haven't you seen five armed men.

(noticing Barrabas)

Oh! Oh!

BARRABAS

What?

TAX COLLECTOR

He seems to recognize me.

BARRABAS

Well?

TAX COLLECTOR

Yes indeed, yes indeed.

(They surround him.)

TAX COLLECTOR

What's he doing? It's you who accompanied me, right?

CAUVIGNAC

Why, yes, Mr. Tax Collector.

TAX COLLECTOR

It was you helped me three days ago when the workers refused the tax. It was you who pulled me from the water when I fell in the river and you did me a proud service, for I do not know how to swim, again, it was you who helped me to fill the King's purse.

CAUVIGNAC

Eh! My God! Yes. It's just what we were saying just now.

TAX COLLECTOR

Ah! I am saved then, ah, my dear friends!

CAUVIGNAC

Saved! Were you by chance running any danger?

TAX COLLECTOR

Damn, you see, at first impression, the absence of Ramoneau and then this disguise.

CAUVIGNAC

What do you mean, this disguise?

TAX COLLECTOR

Yes, this beard—yesterday, your beard was short and black.

CAUVIGNAC

And today it is long and white; I am going to explain to you, my friend.

(he signals his companions while the Tax Collector listens)

Here it is, the heat of a resolve which I took last night made my beard grow more quickly than ordinary—and the anguish which followed on this resolution.

TAX COLLECTOR

Well?

CAUVIGNAC

It made it go white as you see.

TAX COLLECTOR

And what was this resolution?

CAUVIGNAC

I reflected that civil war is a horrible calamity. I reflected that the Queen with her insolence, Monsieur de Mazarin with his avariciousness, the King with the powerlessness of his youth were going to rain a deluge of misfortunes on France.

BARRABAS

Oh! Oh! Oh!

TAX COLLECTOR

Ah! Bah!

CAUVIGNAC

I reflected the Monsieur de Condé, to the contrary, this hero, the conqueror at Rochborg, at Lens, at Fribourd, this cavalier who has saved France from Sprague, can yet from the depths of prison where Mazarin makes him shiver, still save the kingdom from misery and anarchy.

TAX COLLECTOR

With the result that?

CAUVIGNAC

With the result that, after some struggle, after some debate to which our patriotism and conscience carried us—we have abandoned the King's side—right, Lieutenant?

BARRABAS

Alas, yes!

TAX COLLECTOR

Ah! Well, the King is losing brave men and it's a great misfortune for France, a misfortune for which I tremble. Let me cross, quickly, gentlemen.

CAUVIGNAC

They are going to let you cross.

BARRABAS

(aside)

Huh? What's he saying?

CAUVIGNAC

Thus, my friend, you, in a cold sweat, will announce on the other side of the river that my army and myself are now for the Prince.

TAX COLLECTOR

I will announce it, but I am sure no one will believe me.

CAUVIGNAC

Oh! I am sure that they will believe you.

TAX COLLECTOR

No.

CAUVIGNAC

Yes, in fact, when they see you arrive without your saddlebags.

TAX COLLECTOR

What do you mean without my saddlebags? I have my saddlebags.

CAUVIGNAC

Doubtless, but once we've taken them, you won't anymore.

TAX COLLECTOR

What? You will take my money?

CAUVIGNAC

Your money? Never! The King's money, you bet!

TAX COLLECTOR

But sir, this money—

CAUVIGNAC

We have to keep it in our quality, as servants of the Prince. Come, Barrabas, my friend shut these saddlebags in the coffers of Monsieur de Condé.

TAX COLLECTOR

But that's a theft!

CAUVIGNAC

No, it's a seizure.

TAX COLLECTOR

It's piracy!

CAUVIGNAC

No, it's war.

TAX COLLECTOR

I protest.

CAUVIGNAC

It's your right.

(one hears the ferry clock)

What's that?

BARRABAS

Milord, the Duke D'Épernon.

TAX COLLECTOR

Help!

CAUVIGNAC

Close his mouth, Carrotel.

BARRABAS

Where shall we put him? In the cellar?

CAUVIGNAC

With Ramoneau? Not at all! They will conspire together against the Prince.

BARRABAS

Where then?

CAUVIGNAC

Where you wish! What the Devil, invent.

FRIGOTIN

(a key in his hand)

Ah, I've got it.

BARRABAS

What?

FRIGOTIN

The key to the fish shed. We are going to have a famous supper.

BARRABAS

Ah! In the fish shed! That's it. Come Frigotin!

FERGUSON

Alert! Alert!

DUKE

(from the other side)

Hey! Ferryman, didn't you hear the clock?

CAUVIGNAC

Ferguson, go find the travelers.

FERGUSON

I am going, Captain.

(leaving)

Five-man escort, a cape, a gilded hat, an insolent air. It's the Duke in person.

CAUVIGNAC

Attention, gentlemen! Each to his post.

(Carrotel tends the nets. Barrabas and Frigotin, who have shut the tax collector in the fish shed, fish. Cauvignac, who has gone back into the house, adjusts his mask under his false beard.)

(The Duke and his escort enter.)

DUKE

Stay there!

(coming forward)

Where is the man who wrote me?

CAUVIGNAC

(coming out)

Here he is!

DUKE

Masked! And why are you masked?

CAUVIGNAC

So that you won't see my face.

DUKE

Then I know your face?

CAUVIGNAC

No, but having seen it once, you might recognize it.

DUKE

You are frank.

CAUVIGNAC

Yes, when frankness cannot do me any harm.

DUKE

And this frankness goes so far as to reveal the secrets of others?

CAUVIGNAC

Why not, when this revelation can get me something?

DUKE

Singular job you have then!

CAUVIGNAC

Damn! One does what one can, sir. I've been in turn, a monk, a lawyer, a doctor, a partisan, you see that my needs are not caused by a lack of a profession.

DUKE

And, for the moment you are a spy?

CAUVIGNAC

Ah, how badly you interpret my services!

DUKE

It seems to me—

CAUVIGNAC

Sir, I am a faithful subject of His Majesty.

DUKE

Well—and so?

CAUVIGNAC

And, as the Duke d'Épernon serves His Majesty, I naturally felt a great weakness for the Duke of Épernon.

DUKE

And so?

CAUVIGNAC

Then, I said to myself! How is it, the Duke d'Épernon who is still young, who is still a gallant cavalier, who is rich, who is generous, who has all possible qualities—how is it the Duke d'Épernon loves a woman enough to commit stupidities for her?

DUKE

Sir!

CAUVIGNAC

He gives her his money. When he has no more he gives her the King's money; he bought her house in Bordeau, a country house in Leborne—he opens himself up to arrest, assassination even, in coming to see this woman and this woman cheats on him.

DUKE

Sir! Sir! You promised to prove that the Duke is deceived to whoever comes in his name and he sent me.

CAUVIGNAC

Certainly, sir, and I am prepared to give you this proof. But you know against the countersign?

DUKE

(pause)

Against a blank pardon you said it in your letter.

CAUVIGNAC

That's exactly correct.

DUKE

(pause)

And this blank pardon, what will you do with it—once you have it?

CAUVIGNAC

What will I do with it? The devil take me if I know! But I asked for it because it's portable, easy, elastic—perhaps it will never be of use to me, perhaps in a week the Duke will see it returned full of signatures like a commercial note.

DUKE

(aside)

Here's a clown I will hang.

(aloud)

Show me the letter.

CAUVIGNAC

Show me the blank-pardon.

DUKE

Is this really the signature of the Duke?

CAUVIGNAC

Is this really the writing of Mademoselle de Lartigues?

DUKE

Let's have it!

CAUVIGNAC

Let's have it!

DUKE

One moment! How did you obtain this letter?

CAUVIGNAC

Why do you care?

DUKE

Because in these days forgeries are so adroit.

CAUVIGNAC

Come now! A forgery! I'm a gentleman, sir.

DUKE

Then I will beat you up.

CAUVIGNAC

What's that?

DUKE

Nothing. I ask how this letter fell in your hands?

CAUVIGNAC

You persist?

DUKE

I persist.

CAUVIGNAC

I am going to tell you. An itinerant merchant was pointed out to me who furnishes wares to Mademoiselle Nanon de Lartigues as an agent of the Prince. The merchant goes from the little house you see down there to Saint Mikel La Riviere where M. de Canolles lives—that explains to you how he was entrusted with this letter.

DUKE

Yes, but it doesn't explain how from his hands it passed to you.

CAUVIGNAC

Quite naturally, I, in my capacity as a royalist—that was my opinion at the time. I waited for the merchant. Invited him to show me the wares he was carrying. Among these objects was the letter from Mademoiselle Nanon—to Monsieur de Canolles; I opened it, I read it, I became indignant, and I wrote to the Duke d'Épernon, while making an exact copy of the letter which I had passed on to M. de Canolles.

DUKE

With the result that Monsieur de Canolles ought to come this evening.

CAUVIGNAC

Unless the Duke has committed some imprudence. But the letter Monsieur de Canolles has received is not in the hand of Mademoiselle de Lartigues.

CAUVIGNAC

I added in the postscript that for greater security, that Mademoiselle de Lartigues used a strange hand.

DUKE

You have foreseen everything.

CAUVIGNAC

It's true, I have a great deal of foresight.

DUKE

I ask your pardon if I continue to interrupt you.

CAUVIGNAC

But, sir! It's a very great honor for me.

DUKE

You just said something that makes me reflect—

CAUVIGNAC

What did I say, sir?

DUKE

You said: "In my capacity as a royalist—which was my opinion at the time." You haven't always been of the same opinion?

CAUVIGNAC

Indeed.

DUKE

But now—are you for the King or the Prince?

CAUVIGNAC

I am neither for the Prince, nor for the King.

DUKE

Then who are you for?

CAUVIGNAC

I am for myself.

DUKE

How, for yourself? Explain this to me, a little, I beg you.

CAUVIGNAC

Ah, it's very easy. Cardinal Mazarin right now, is making war for the Queen; you make war for the King. I am making war for myself.

DUKE

Meaning—I am doing business with a partisan leader?

CAUVIGNAC

Oh, my God, yes.

DUKE

A captain of bandits?

CAUVIGNAC

Exactly.

DUKE

And didn't you think of one thing?

CAUVIGNAC

What?

DUKE

That, after making such an admission to me—

CAUVIGNAC

Well?

DUKE

An idea might come to me?

CARROTEL

What idea?

DUKE

The idea of arresting you.

CAUVIGNAC

In fact, I did think of it.

DUKE

And?

CAUVIGNAC

I've taken all my precautions.

DUKE

All your precautions?

CAUVIGNAC

All! Have a look over there! Hop!

(Barrabas, Carrotel, Ferguson, and Frigotin raise their weapons at the Duke's five-man escort.)

DUKE

Ah!

CAUVIGNAC

(drawing a pistol from his belt)

Now, look over here.

DUKE

Ah! Ah!

DUKE'S GUARD

Eh! Others! Eh! What the devil are you doing?

CAUVIGNAC

Nothing, nothing! Retire my boys.

(makes a sign and his men vanish)

DUKE

Here's your blank-pass.

CAUVIGNAC

Here's your letter.

DUKE

Thank you, sir. But if we were to meet again, you won't find it wrong if—

CAUVIGNAC

If you hang me? What, Duke? Only catching comes before hanging and I will do my best not to give you this little satisfaction.

DUKE

(to his guard)

Come on—

(He leaves. The guards follow him.)

CAUVIGNAC

Bon voyage! Duke! Bon voyage, gentlemen. We won't meet again.

CAUVIGNAC

Come here, everybody.

ALL

Here we are.

CAUVIGNAC

What did I promise you? Gold and a guarantee! The guarantee! Here! The gold here!

ALL

And now, as the Duke has promised to hang us if he meets us again, I think it wouldn't be bad to leave.

BARRABAS

Let's get going!

FERRYMAN

(from the cellar)

Hey, what about me?

CAUVIGNAC

It's true!

BARRABAS

Ah! And the Tax Collector.

CAUVIGNAC

He's right—pull the Tax Collector from the fish shed, while I release the Ferryman from the cellar—hurry, come, you.

FERRYMAN

(leaving)

Ah!

CAUVIGNAC

Are you happy?

FERRYMAN

I am happy—and my gold piece?

CAUVIGNAC

Here it is.

FERRYMAN

My word, it's good money.

CAUVIGNAC

I should think so—it's the King's money.

BARRABAS

Captain! Captain!

CAUVIGNAC

What?

BARRABAS

The Tax Collector is no longer in the fish shed.

FERRYMAN

What, in the shed? You put the Tax Collector in the shed?.

BARRABAS

He's not there anymore.

FERRYMAN

I should think so. There's no bottom of the tank.

CAUVIGNAC

We've drowned a Tax Collector. Save yourself if you can.

ALL

Save yourself, if you can.

CURTAIN

ACT I
SCENE 2

A hall in an inn. In a cut away at the right, a large window giving on the highway. In another cut away a stairway leading to the upstairs rooms. To the left another window.

The Vicomtess de Cambes is at the top of the staircase, dressed elegantly in male attire.

FRANCINETTE

You heard, Mr. Biscarros, a pretty supper, the best you have— in a word, like the last, you know.

BISCARROS

And for what time, my beautiful child?

FRANCINETTE

For ten, precisely.

BISCARROS

It will be ready. Who will call for it?

FRANCINETTE

But it seems to me, you know the house since it can be seen from here. Bring the supper—you will be paid in advance even—if you wish it.

BISCARROS

Eh! My God, Mademoiselle Francinette, you know indeed that it is not for money, but still—

FRANCINETTE

What?

BISCARROS

One likes to know who one is serving.

FRANCINETTE

Well, you are serving my mistress, a young widow, twenty-two or twenty-three years old, blonde, pretty, and giving a supper twice a week. It seems to me that is all you need to know. Goodbye, Master Biscarros.

BISCARROS

Ah! Mademoiselle Francinette!

(He runs after her)

THE VICOMTESS

(going down the staircase to the window)

Still no one! Truly, I begin to think that something bad may have happened to this poor Richon.

BISCARROS

(returning)

Ah, pardon, sir, I didn't see you.

THE VICOMTESS

It's that I came in while you were talking with that pretty girl.

BISCARROS

Ah! Young man! Young man!

THE VICOMTESS

Well?

BISCARROS

(bowing respectfully)

Your table is set, sir.

(He indicates a table)

THE VICOMTESS

(sitting)

You know quite well, I don't eat alone, and that I am waiting for a companion. When he arrives, you can prepare your meal.

BISCARROS

Ah, sir, it's not to criticize your friend, he is certainly free to come or not to come, but it's a very bad habit to make one wait.

THE VICOMTESS

(rising and going to the window)

Myself, you see, I am astonished that he is so late.

BISCARROS

And I, I am more than astonished, I am pained.

THE VICOMTESS

You—and for what reason?

BISCARROS

The roast is going to be burned.

THE VICOMTESS

Take it from the spit.

BISCARROS

Then it will be cold.

THE VICOMTESS

Put something else on the fire.

BISCARROS

The other won't be cooked.

THE VICOMTESS

In that case, do as you wish, my friend, I abandon the thing to your profound wisdom.

BISCARROS

Eh! Sir, there's no wisdom, my friend, not even that of King Solomon which can make a reheated meal edible.

(He leaves in despair.)

THE VICOMTESS

(alone returning from the side of the window)

Poor devil! I truly believe that he regards this as a great misfortune. Ah, it seems to me, I see someone. Is it him? No, Richon must come alone, I see two men. Oh! Oh! Who are they then? they're going in the woods. They're hiding behind the branches—I saw them light a musket. Do they want my two treasures, gold pieces. No, for in supposing that Richon arrives this evening and that I can go to Lebourn, that is to say far away from the corner where these men are lying in ambush.

POMPEY

(appears on the stairway)

Sir! Sir!

THE VICOMTESS

Ah, it's you, Pompey.

POMPEY

Hush!

THE VICOMTESS

What's wrong?

POMPEY

I'm watching while you are here.

THE VICOMTESS

Fine, Pompey, fine. And what have you seen?

POMPEY

An ambush is in preparation.

THE VICOMTESS

An ambush!

POMPEY

Trust an old soldier.

THE VICOMTESS

I trust you more, my brave Pompey, since I have seen what you have seen.

POMPEY

Two men, right?

THE VICOMTESS

Two men, yes. And two others here.

POMPEY

(coming down the stairs)

More?

THE VICOMTESS

Only, those are hiding on the other side of the road.

POMPEY

Ambush! Ambush! I believe we won't do badly to barricade ourselves, sir, although the house is poorly built to withstand a siege. During this time, we will send for help at Lebourn.

THE VICOMTESS

Pompey, my dear Pompey, you forget one thing—it is that, Lebourn is full of the Queen's troops and that we serve Madame de Condé.

POMPEY

That's exactly correct.

THE VICOMTESS

And yet, who told you that they are after us?

POMPEY

Sir, when one is on campaign, you must always have an eye on the enemy.

THE VICOMTESS

Wait, we are going to learn what enemy they are after.

POMPEY

In any case, I am going to put myself in readiness.

(He takes a musket and walks about ferociously at the top of the staircase.)

THE VICOMTESS

(sitting by the table)

Master Biscarros! Master Biscarros!

(Biscarros enters.)

BISCARROS

(sticking his head around the door)

Did you call me, sir? Do you perchance see your companion coming?

THE VICOMTESS

No, but I have some information to ask of you.

(Biscarros enters holding a half plucked chicken.)

POMPEY

Hum! Hum!

BISCARROS

Huh?

THE VICOMTESS

Pay no attention—you know the neighborhood, right?

BISCARROS

Certainly. I am from these parts.

THE VICOMTESS

Well, I want to ask you, if there's no indiscretion in my asking, to whom does that little house belong that can be seen down there?

BISCARROS

Devil! Devil!

THE VICOMTESS

Ah—it appears.

BISCARROS

No, but you see, I can't tell you what I don't know myself.

THE VICOMTESS

That's very true—in any case, it must belong to a woman for just now I saw her appear on her balcony.

BISCARROS

And a charming woman, a widow.

THE VICOMTESS

A widow.

BISCARROS

(mysteriously)

But the shade of her first husband, and even of her second come visit her from time to time. Only there's one strange thing—the shades agree between themselves probably and never come the same day or rather the same night.

POMPEY

Hum! Hum!

THE VICOMTESS

Fine, Pompey, fine! Well, there may be an apparition this evening, Master Biscarros.

BISCARROS

I would be tempted to believe it, because the chamber maid, this pretty girl you just saw here, came to command a fine supper at ten p.m.

THE VICOMTESS

And to whom does the lady widow give a supper this evening?

BISCARROS

To one of the two shades probably.

THE VICOMTESS

Have you ever seen these two shades?

BISCARROS

One is a shade of fifty-five to sixty years and he seems to me to have the air of her first husband for he comes openly, like a shade sure of the priority of his rights.

THE VICOMTESS

And the other?

BISCARROS

The other is that of a young man of twenty-four or twenty-five years, and I must say it, he is more timid, and has the air of a soul in pain—I would swear it is the soul of her second husband.

THE VICOMTESS

And that, because—?

BISCARROS

Because it comes here, stops, looks, explores the woods, the ravines, the plains, still I understand.

THE VICOMTESS

And which of the two shades is expected today?

BISCARROS

Give me your hand, Vicomte.

(leading her to the other window)

Look—hush!

(He retires smiling.)

THE VICOMTESS

This young man who is coming on horseback?

BISCARROS

Hush!

THE VICOMTESS

He's the shade of her second husband?

BISCARROS

(as he leaves)

Hush.

THE VICOMTESS

Pompey!

POMPEY

(taken by surprise)

Huh?

THE VICOMTESS

Close the trunk, and have everything ready for our departure.

POMPEY

And the ambush?

THE VICOMTESS

It's not us they are after.

POMPEY

Ah, damn! You've done well to tell me that—the mustard was burning my nose, and although it would have been an unpardonable impudence I was going to make a sortie.

THE VICOMTESS

Well, my brave Pompey, instead make a reentry and get ready.

(Pompey goes back in the room.)

THE VICOMTESS

(alone)

Now, I understand everything. The young woman on the balcony is awaiting the chevalier from Lebourn. The faceless men in the woods plan to attack the visitor. Ah, here's one who comes out and goes back to hiding. He makes a sign to others. That's it, indeed. They have seen him the poor young man! They know his heart is down there, that he must make his body go where his heart awaits him. He's hurrying, carelessly, joyously, without realizing that between him and the one he loves lies a danger. For this ambush, these man armed with muskets. It's death perhaps—oh, it is impossible to allow this to happen before my eyes. But what to do? Stop the young man that I do not know? Here he is, he's going to pass by—he's passing by (calling) sir!

CANOLLES

(outside)

What?

THE VICOMTESS

Here—stop, please—yes, yes, come here, over here, this way—I have something of importance to say to you.

CANOLLES

I'm here at your orders, sir—what can I do for you, sir?

THE VICOMTESS

Come here, sir, come here, more, for I have something to tell
you that cannot be said too loudly. There, now put your hat on
your head, for it must be seen that we have known each other for
a long while—and that it is I you came to see at this inn.

CANOLLES

But, sir, I don't understand.

THE VICOMTESS

You will soon. Give me your hand. That's right! Enchanted to
see you, sir. Now, don't leave this inn or you are lost.

CANOLLES

Oh! Oh! What's wrong then? Were you set in my way—by—?

THE VICOMTESS

By Providence, yes, Monsieur.

CANOLLES

At least you will explain to me?

THE VICOMTESS

Put your horse in the stable and come rejoin me here.

CANOLLES

Castorin, you hear!

(He climbs through the window.)

THE VICOMTESS

Well, what are you doing?

CANOLLES

Damn, you appear to be in a hurry to speak to me—so I'm taking the shortcut.

THE VICOMTESS

Oh, sir, sir, I am very much afraid that with all these imprudences—

CANOLLES

I am guilty of imprudence? Truly, I don't doubt it. Well, now we are alone, tell me, sir, what is going on.

THE VICOMTESS

It's that you were going to that little house down there—where the light shines.

CANOLLES

I?

THE VICOMTESS

You were going there. Don't deny it, but on the route to that house, on the way side, in the somber shadows four men are lying in ambush.

CANOLLES

Four men are in ambush—and who are they waiting for?

THE VICOMTESS

You!

CANOLLES

Ah—and you are sure?

THE VICOMTESS

I saw them arrive two-by-two and hide themselves—two in the rocks two in the trees. Then, when just now you appeared on the road, one of the two made a sign and—

CANOLLES

And?

THE VICOMTESS

And I heard muskets being cocked.

CANOLLES

Plague! The heroes!

THE VICOMTESS

You may laugh. It's just as I tell you, and if the night wasn't dark, you could perhaps see them and recognize them.

CANOLLES

Ah, after what you tell me, I have no need to see them to recognize them. I know who they are to a marvel. But, you, sir, who told you I was going to this little house and that it was I they were waiting for?

THE VICOMTESS

I divined it, sir.

CANOLLES

You are a very charming person, sir. Ah, they wanted to shoot me. And how many are there involved in this loveable operation?

THE VICOMTESS

Four!

CANOLLES

Oh—there must be a chief!

THE VICOMTESS

Older than the others—fifty-five to sixty, round shoulders, braided hat, white feather.

CANOLLES

The Duke of Épernon.

THE VICOMTESS

The Governor of Guyenne?

CANOLLES

Fine! Look how I tell you my business; I've never done it to others. But never mind, you've done me a great enough service that I won't look too closely. So, it's agreed.

(holding out his hand)

You saved my life.

THE VICOMTESS

Oh, sir, you are exaggerating the service I've done you.

CANOLLES

No, on my honor, it is as I told you. I know the Duke, he's devil-ishly brutal. As to you, my young savior, you are a model of perspicacity, a type of Christian charity. But tell me, had you gone so far as to warn—?

THE VICOMTESS

Where?

CANOLLES

Down there in the little house.

THE VICOMTESS

How would that be possible for me? I've only been here two hours—I don't know anyone.

CANOLLES

It's that she's waiting for me—poor Nanon!

THE VICOMTESS

Nanon! Nanon de Lartigues?

CANOLLES

Ah, what's all this mean? You see some men lying in ambush on the road, you divine whom they are after; I mention a baptismal name and you say the family name. You are a sorcerer, admit it or if not, I'll denounce you and have you condemned to burn by the Parliament at Bordeaux.

THE VICOMTESS

Oh, this time you will admit it's unnecessary to be a sorcerer to ferret you out. Once you had denounced the Duke d'Épernon as your rival, it was evident that if you named some Nanon, it was Nanon de Lartigues.

CANOLLES

You know her?

THE VICOMTESS

What a suggestion!

CANOLLES

Oh—don't get shocked. Nanon is a charming woman—full of
fidelity to her promises, so much so that she takes pleasure in
keeping them, completely devoted to the one she loves for as
long as she loves that lucky person. I want to dine with her this
evening, but the Duke has spoiled the party. Let's not speak
any more of it, tomorrow the Duke will leave and if you wish,
tomorrow I will present you to her!

THE VICOMTESS

Thanks, sir, I only know Mademoiselle de Lartigues by name
and do not wish to know her further.

CANOLLES

And you are wrong, by God! Nanon. Nanon is a good girl to
know in every respect.

THE VICOMTESS

But, while waiting, sir, there is a woman horribly compromised
and who, if she isn't warned—

CANOLLES

You are right, my young friend and I forgot, in the charm of
your conversation, my duties of a gentleman. Look, you know
in actual war, when force won't work, my must employ a ruse—
help me to devise a ruse.

THE VICOMTESS

I ask nothing better; but what kind?

CANOLLES

Wait—the inn has two doors.

THE VICOMTESS

I know nothing of that.

CANOLLES

Well, I know—one gives on the great highway—the other on the country side. I will describe a half circle and I am going to rap on Nanon's door—her house also has a rear door.

THE VICOMTESS

Yes, so you can be surprised in the house!

CANOLLES

I will only enter for a short time and then leave.

THE VICOMTESS

If you once enter, you will never leave again.

CANOLLES

Decidedly, you are a magician.

THE VICOMTESS

Also, it will be even worse—for you will probably be slain before her eyes.

CANOLLES

Bah! There are some closets.

THE VICOMTESS

Oh, sir—

CANOLLES

Ah—are you a Knight of Malta or by chance are you destined for the church?

THE VICOMTESS

In fact, you are right, sir—go ahead! For in truth, I don't know why I am meddling in this—go ahead! But hide yourself carefully.

CANOLLES

Well, I'm wrong and it's you who are right. But how to warn her, by God?

THE VICOMTESS

A letter, it seems to me.

CANOLLES

Doubtless a letter. But who will carry it to her?

THE VICOMTESS

I thought you'd seen a lackey—in such circumstances, a lackey only risks a few blows with a stick while a gentleman risks his life.

CANOLLES

Truly, I am losing my mind—and Castorin, as you just said, will do the job wonderfully.

(going up and calling)

Master Biscarros! Master Biscarros!

(Biscarros shows his head)

CANOLLES

Some paper, ink and a pen—then send me my lackey.

(Biscarros leaves.)

CANOLLES

Now, sir, I hope you will be so gracious as to tell me to whom I owe thanks for such good advice?

THE VICOMTESS

Sir, I am the Vicomtess de Cambes.

CANOLLES

Ah good! I had heard a charming Vicomtess de Cambes spoken of—who has a good number of lands in the vicinity of Fort Saint Georges—and who is friends with the Princess.

THE VICOMTESS

That is my beautiful sister.

CANOLLES

Ah, my word, I give you my compliment, Vicomte—I hope that if the occasion favors me, you will present me to her—I am the Baron de Canolles, Captain in Navailles, and moreover, your very thankful servant.

THE VICOMTESS

You are the Baron de Canolles?

CANOLLES

You know me?

THE VICOMTESS

By reputation only.

CANOLLES

And a bad reputation, isn't it?

THE VICOMTESS

Oh!

CANOLLES

What do you expect? Each follows his nature—I live an agitated life.

THE VICOMTESS

You are perfectly free to live as you choose, Baron.

(Biscarros enters with paper, pen, and ink.)

THE VICOMTESS

But they are bringing you what you need to write with.

CANOLLES

(going to the table)

Thanks.

(aside)

A very singular little fellow.

(to Biscarros)

And my servant?

BISCARROS

He's coming, sir.

(The Countess makes signs to Biscarros while Canolles writes.)

THE VICOMTESS

No one has come?

BISCARROS

No one.

CANOLLES

Huh? What did you say, Master Biscarros?

BISCARROS

Nothing! I am preparing the supper menu with this gentleman.

CANOLLES

Bravo!

(still writing)

Would you like to join me, Vicomte?

THE VICOMTESS

Impossible, Monsieur de Canolles—I am expecting someone.

CANOLLES

(aside)

Decidedly, his respectable father must have raised him in horror of the Canolles.

(He writes.)

THE VICOMTESS

If the person I am expecting arrives, don't let him come in, but warn me.

BISCARROS

It will be done as you wish. But let him hurry—or the supper—

THE VICOMTESS

Go, Master Biscarros.

(Biscarros leaves. Meanwhile, Castorin has entered and take a position near his master.)

CANOLLES

Ah, you are there!

CASTORIN

Yes, sir.

CANOLLES

Castorin, you know that for this evening, the campaign is over.

CASTORIN

What do you say, sir?

CANOLLES

For me, but not for you, come here—and tell me how far you've gotten with Mademoiselle Francinette.

CASTORIN

But sir, I don't know if I ought to—

CANOLLES

Rest easy, master stupid, I have no intentions about her.

CASTORIN

In that case, sir—it's another matter.

CANOLLES

Speak then.

CASTORIN

Mademoiselle Francinette has the intelligence to appreciate my qualities.

CANOLLES

You are in good with her, right, Mr. Lackey? Very good, take this letter then and go by way of the meadow.

CASTORIN

I know the road.

CANOLLES

That's true! Go knock at the service entrance. Doubtless you know this door.

CASTORIN

Perfectly.

CANOLLES

And deliver this letter to Mademoiselle Francinette.

CASTORIN

(after starting to leave)

Ah, pardon, sir.

CANOLLES

Now what?

CASTORIN

Suppose they don't open the door to me by chance?

CANOLLES

Then you will be a fool, and in this case I will be a gentleman with the right to complain of having a beggar such as you in my service. But you have a special way of knocking I am sure.

CASTORIN

Oh, yes, sir, I have one—I strike first two times at equal intervals then.

CANOLLES

I do not ask you how you rap—little concern to me so long as they open to you. Go then, and if you are surprised eat the paper or I'll cut off your ears when you return—if it hasn't already been done—well—why aren't you on your way?

CASTORIN

In fact, sir, in fact.

CANOLLES

Well—what are you doing?

CASTORIN

Sir.

CANOLLES

You know very well it isn't for this door, but by that one.

CASTORIN

It's true.

(He leaves by the door at the right, meanwhile, the Vicomtess who has been talking at the door in the rear with the Biscarros, returns.)

THE VICOMTESS

And now, Baron.

CANOLLES

Here I am, Vicomte, have you more advice to give me?

THE VICOMTESS

No, but I have a prayer to make to you.

CANOLLES

Which is?

THE VICOMTESS

It's to pick the corner you prefer to dine in, since not having any special preference, if you wish to remain here—

CANOLLES

Well?

THE VICOMTESS

I will slip into another room.

CANOLLES

Ah—ah—that means—?

THE VICOMTESS

It means that the person I've been expecting has arrived.

CANOLLES

And that you wish to rid yourself of Baron de Canolles.

THE VICOMTESS

Oh! Baron—

CANOLLES

Vicomte, you were the first here, the table was taken here for you. It is right for me to retire.

BISCARROS

The Baron's supper is served in the side room.

CANOLLES

All the same, it's not very nice to send me away and let me dine alone like a pauper so that your companion, your friend, your unknown remains an unknown—in which case, you understand, although having offered to escort you to Nanon's,—you can indeed, in your turn—no. Very frankly, Vicomte, let's not speak of it anymore.

Master Biscarros, how much do all these geese cost that are in the window?

BISCARROS

Only three pistoles.

CANOLLES

Here are three pistoles—go on ahead and if there's something to say about your supper, you will come that way.

(He goes out.)

BISCARROS

Oh—I have no fear of that, sir.

(He goes out.)

THE VICOMTESS

(going quickly to the door)

Come in, Richon!

RICHON

We are observed, it appears.

THE VICOMTESS

No, not precisely—but as I was with a gentleman who seemed to me to be rather too indiscreet, I took my precautions.

RICHON

And he is—?

THE VICOMTESS

There, in the next room.

RICHON

What's his name?

THE VICOMTESS

The Baron de Canolles.

RICHON

Ah! That's right—they told me, that the beautiful Nanon de

Lartigues lives in this neighborhood.

THE VICOMTESS

Here—not five hundred feet from this inn.

RICHON

That explains the presence of Baron de Canolles at the Golden Calf Inn.

THE VICOMTESS

You know him?

RICHON

Who? The Baron? Yes, I could even say that I am his friend, if Monsieur de Canolles wasn't of an excellent nobility while I am only a poor commoner.

THE VICOMTESS

A commoner like you, Richon, is more valuable than a prince in the situation we are in.

RICHON

Are you sure you were not recognized by him?

THE VICOMTESS

It's not easy to recognize those you've never seen.

RICHON

What I meant to say was figured out?

(Biscarros enters with a plate which he puts on the table.)

THE VICOMTESS

In fact, he looked at me a lot.

RICHON

I believe that! You don't often meet gentleman of your description—that's fine, Master Biscarros—go! if we have need of something, we will call.

THE VICOMTESS

He's a happy cavalier, the Baron, it strikes me—

RICHON

Happy and good—a charming wit and a great heart. Gascons you know are never mediocre—either all good or all bad—this one is excellent in love as in war—at once a fop and a brave captain—I am disappointed that he works against us. Truly, you really ought to have tried to win him over to our cause since chance put him in your way.

THE VICOMTESS

What! That scatter-brain?

RICHON

Eh! My God are we so serious and so reasonable, we, who in our impudent hands light the torch of civil war as if it were a candle in a church? Is it a man quite as serious as Cardinal Mazarin, son of a fisherman from Piscina, who becomes Prime Minister not from ambition, but avarice? Is it a woman quite so serious as Madame de Condé who even yesterday was only occupied with dresses, jewels, diamonds, and who today commands her own cavalry and engages in a coup d'état? Is it the leader of a faction as serious as the Duke d'Épernon who still plays clown and who just put on his first long pants, who disturbs all France? Still, I myself am a person so grave—the son of a miller from Angoulême, the former servant of Monsieur de la Rochefoucauld to whom, one day, my master gave a sword which I bear bravely at my side, imitating a man of war? And now, here's the son of a miller from Angouleme become a Captain, this one's going to be a colonel, a governor of a province—who knows what? He will perhaps hold for ten minutes, an hour, a day even, the destiny of a kingdom in his hands, you see this very much resembles a dream, and yet I take it for a reality until the day some great catastrophe awakens me.

THE VICOMTESS

And on that day, misfortune to those who wake you—Richon! For you will be a hero!

(She escorts him to the table.)

RICHON

A hero or a traitor depending on whether we are the stronger or the weaker.

THE VICOMTESS

True! But on what food have you been eating today, that you see everything for the worst, my dear Richon? Civil war is a sad thing, I am aware, but sometimes necessary.

RICHON

Yes, necessary—like the plague! Oh, you women don't understand war! You only see an ocean of intrigues and you plunge right in as if it were your natural element. And yet, I said the other day to Her Highness, Madame de Condé, and she agreed with me, women live in a sphere from which the artillery shots that kill us seem to you no more than child's play.

THE VICOMTESS

Truly, you frighten me, Richon, and if I weren't sure of having you there to protect me, I would no longer dare to put myself en route.

(giving him her hand)

But it's useless for you to talk—under your escort, I fear nothing.

RICHON

Ah—my escort—that's right, you made me think of it—you must leave my protection—Vicomte.

THE VICOMTESS

What's that?

RICHON

The game is broken off.

THE VICOMTESS

But shouldn't you return with me to Chantilly?

RICHON

It's true I ought to remain as I am not needed here. But as I told you just now my importance has increased so much, I have received from the Princess an order not to leave the neighborhood of the Fort de Vayres—on which it appears they have some designs.

THE VICOMTESS

Oh, my God—what are you saying to me, Richon! To leave without you—to leave with this worthy Pompey who in pretending to be brave, and is a hundred times more of a poltroon than I am—crossing half of France alone or nearly so? Oh no; I will not leave—I swear it! I will die of fear before getting there.

RICHON

That's your fantasy, Vicomtess, now take care! They are counting on you in Chantilly, and princes are not slow to lose patience, especially when they are waiting for money—speaking of money, are you really rich? I ask your pardon, but it's a question they've strongly recommended that I ask you.

THE VICOMTESS

Not at all; I have great trouble to get from my farmer twenty thousand pounds—which I have with me—in gold—that's all I've got.

RICHON

That's all! Plague! How you go on! To speak with such scorn of such a sum at such a moment. Twenty thousand pounds—you are not as rich as Cardinal Mazarin, but you are richer than the King.

THE VICOMTESS

So you think this humble offering will be accepted?

RICHON

With thanks! You are bringing Madame de Condé enough to pay an army.

THE VICOMTESS

And you say that they are waiting for this money impatiently?

RICHON

Yes, and if I had advice to give you, it's to leave this very evening.

THE VICOMTESS

This evening. At night?

RICHON

So much the better—the more obscure it is, the less they can see you are afraid—and you will meet more poltroons than you— that you are well put to flight—besides, there are soldiers of the King around here and we are not yet at war.

(Vicomtess and Richon rise. Pompey comes in and comes forward.)

THE VICOMTESS

You are right, I am leaving. Don't you have some particular commissions for His Highness?

RICHON

Ah, I believe I do! You remind me of the most important.

THE VICOMTESS

You've written it?

RICHON

No—there are only two words to transmit.

THE VICOMTESS

Which are?

RICHON

Bordeau! Yes!

THE VICOMTESS

She will understand what this means?

RICHON

Perfectly! And sure of these two words, she can leave in perfect confidence.

THE VICOMTESS

(to Pompey who is listening)

Let's go, Pompey.

POMPEY

What, Vicomte, sir?

THE VICOMTESS

We've got to leave, my friend.

POMPEY

To leave? But there's going to be a frightful storm.

RICHON

What the devil are you talking about, Pompey? There's not a cloud in the sky.

POMPEY

But during the night, we could mistake the way.

RICHON

That would be difficult; you have only to follow the main road and there's a magnificent moon out.

POMPEY

Moonlight, moonlight—you understand that it's not for me that I am saying this, Monsieur Richon.

RICHON

By God—an old soldier.

POMPEY

When one has fought the Spaniards and been wounded in the battle of Corbie—

RICHON

One has no more fear of anything—well, this falls out wonderfully since the Vicomte is not reassured at all.

POMPEY

(to Vicomtess)

Oh! Oh! You're afraid.

THE VICOMTESS

Not with you, my brave Pompey—for I know you, and I know that you will be killed before they get to me.

POMPEY

Doubtless—so now if you are too frightened we must wait until tomorrow.

THE VICOMTESS

Impossible, my brave Pompey. Here, place this gold in the saddle bags of your horse, I will rejoin you in a moment.

POMPEY

That's a gross sum to expose at night.

THE VICOMTESS

There's no danger, or little, Richon said. Let's see: are the pistols in their holster, the sword in its scabbard, and the musket on its hook?

POMPEY

You forget, Vicomte sir, that when one has been a soldier all his life he never leaves anything to chance. Yes, sir, each thing is in its place.

RICHON

See if one can be afraid with such a companion?

POMPEY

(to Vicomtess)

What about that ambush?

THE VICOMTESS

We will turn our back on them. And besides, they were on foot.

POMPEY

And we are on horseback—I am going to give mine a double ration of hay.

(He leaves.)

RICHON

Bon voyage Vicomte!

THE VICOMTESS

Thanks for the thought; but it's a long way! Oh, bother! Isn't our Baron going to notice my departure?

RICHON

Oh, at that moment, he has something to do—meaning have his dinner—and if his is as good as ours it's unlikely he'll leave his table without a strong motive—besides, I am staying here, and I will keep him.

THE VICOMTESS

Then make him my excuse for my impoliteness to him. I do not wish to—if I meet him one day in a less generous mood than he was in today he would pick a quarrel—he's so refined, your Baron.

RICHON

You said the word—he's a man to follow you to the ends of the Earth for nothing but to cross swords with you—but be easy, I will pay him your compliments.

THE VICOMTESS

Fine—goodbye, Richon—

(returning)

Say, I am thinking what you said just now—if this Canolles is as brave a captain and as fine a gentleman as you say.

RICHON

Well?

THE VICOMTESS

Why not attempt to enlist him in our cause? He could rejoin us—be it at Chantilly, be it during the voyage. Knowing him a little already, I could introduce him.

(Richon smiles)

As to the rest, I take it I have said nothing, and do what you think best. Goodbye! Goodbye!

(She leaves.)

RICHON

(alone)

Go enlarge this council of women that men are mad enough to obey! Go toss in a new germ of hate or love in the midst of this world of passions! War of Women, War of Women—oh, how the people in their sovereign wisdom have aptly named this strange war we are waging.

CANOLLES

(entering gaily)

Ah—there, my little gentleman—hold on, it seems to me he's grown since our separation. Say there, Vicomte, ah, excuse me, it's not you—but it is death of my life—it's Richon, a friend of ten years for a friend of two hours. Ah, by God! You arrive happily.

RICHON

Good day, Baron. In what way am I so welcome?

CANOLLES

I needed to find someone to whom to praise Master Biscarros, not even having that clown Castorin that I sent on an errand that will get his bones broken. Have you eaten like us? Listen to the menu—bisque, hors d'oeuvres, marinated oysters, anchovies and caviar, capon in olives with a bottle of Medoc—you'll find it's cadaver on the field of battle down there—young partridge stuffed with truffles, peas, caramel, a cherry jelly, all washed down with a bottle of Cambertin like the Médoc. What's more, the dessert—Ah, but it seems to me you have not been badly treated. A bottle of Ermitage, a little the worse for wear, by God!

(going to the table)

Richon, it must have been like the others. Ah, I am in a fine humor, and Master Biscarros is a great master.

(coming to Richon and forcing him to sit at the table)

Sit there, Richon. You've eaten; well—I too have eaten. What's that prove? We shall start over.

RICHON

Thanks, Baron—I am no longer hungry.

CANOLLES

(pouring wine to drink)

I admit that, strictly speaking, one may not be hungry but one must always be thirsty. Taste some of this Ermitage—so you dined, dined with the little rascal of a Vicomte? Not at all, I am mistaken, dear friend, he's a charming boy, to whom I owe the pleasure of savoring life by his handsome side instead of delivering my soul through the three or four holes that the brave Duke d'Épernon counted on putting in my skin. I am indebted to him, to this handsome young Vicomte, this ravishing Ganymede—oh, Richon, Richon, you have indeed the air of being what they say you are—that is a true servant of Monsieur de Condé.

RICHON

Come now, Baron—not sharing these ideas, you will make me die with laughter.

CANOLLES

(listening to galloping horses)

Eh! What's that?

RICHON

I think I know.

CANOLLES

Say it, then.

RICHON

It's our little gentleman leaving.

CANOLLES

Without bidding me adieu? Decidedly, he's a crank.

FERRYMAN

Not at all, my dear Baron, he's a man in a hurry that's all.

CANOLLES

What singular manners! How was this boy brought up? I would be capable of destroying the home of his tutor, Richon, my friend—I foresaw he'd do you wrong. Things aren't done this way by gentlemen. By God, I think if I caught him, I'd pull his ears.

RICHON

Don't get angry—the Vicomte is not so badly brought up as you believe, for, when he was parting from me, he charged me to express all his apologies to you—and to flatter you a thousand times.

CANOLLES

Fine, fine—holy water of court which makes a great impertinence a small act of impoliteness. By god, I am in a ferocious mood—pick a quarrel with me Richon—you don't wish to? By God, listen Richon my friend, I find you very ugly.

RICHON

With such a mood, Baron, you will be, if we gamble, capable of winning a 100 pistoles from me, this evening—fate favors those greatly chagrined you know.

CANOLLES

(going to the rear and shouting)

Cards! Ah, by God, Gambling—you are right, my friend. That's an idea that reconciles me to you. Richon, you are as beautiful as Adonis, and I pardon Monsieur de Cambes—Biscarros, some cards.

RICHON

No, no—it's not worth the trouble my friend.

CANOLLES

Why not worth the trouble?

RICHON

You see, I haven't got the time to play.

CANOLLES

No time to play, no time to drink.

RICHON

Dear Baron, I have some very pressing business.

CANOLLES

And you are leaving me?

RICHON

I am leaving you!

(going to get his hat and his sword)

CANOLLES

Ah, damn, but I am going to be horribly bored here all alone.
I haven't the least wish to sleep. Suppose I proposed to accompany you, Baron?

RICHON

I would refuse that honor, Baron. The business with which I am
involved is of a type that admits no witnesses.

CANOLLES

Very well—you are acting for which side?

RICHON

I was going to beg you not to ask me that question.

CANOLLES

To which side has that Vicomte gone?

RICHON

I must answer you that I do not know.

CANOLLES

My dear Richon, you are quite full of mysteries this evening, but you are completely at liberty. A last glass and goodbye!

RICHON

To our health and goodbye.

(Richon leaves.)

CANOLLES

(alone)

Bon voyage! Oh damn! What the devil is there against me in this damn country? Some of them are chasing after me to kill me, the others flee as if I had the plague. By God! I'm no longer hungry. I feel I'm getting depressed. I am capable of getting as drunk as a German. Hey, Castorin, come here so I can beat you up. What the devil can Richon have to do with this impertinent little Vicomte, and where do these comings and goings, this air of mystery come from? Ah, double damn—they're conspiring—that's it. That explains everything to me. Now, for whom do they conspire? Is it for the Parliament? Is it for the King? Is it for the Queen? Is it for Cardinal Mazarin? Is it for the Madame de Condé? My word, it's all the same to me. I'm getting thirsty again.

(pouring himself a drink)

But Richon, to conspire with a child of sixteen, with—

(noticing a glove that the Vicomtess dropped)

Here, what's this? His glove—a pretty little glove, my word, scented, elegant, embroidered—embroidered like a woman's glove.

(trying to put it on)

Wow! What kind of hand is this? It's impossible that a man could wear such a glove. Oh triple fool that you are Canolles—that blush, that reserve, the refusal to dine with me, those delicacies on behalf of poor Nanon—he's a woman! A woman! Ah, for goodness sake, Madame, you will allow me—what the devil! When they save your life you get involved. Biscarros! Castorin! Biscarros!

CASTORIN

(coming in the side door)

Ah, sir! Help. Murder! Assassination.

CANOLLES

Castorin! Come here!

CASTORIN

Oh, sir, Monsieur d'Épernon's swagger stick beat unmercifully.

CANOLLES

(writing)

Very fine!

CASTORIN

Sir, what do you mean, very fine? I was not able to deliver your letter.

CANOLLES

Very fine!

CASTORIN

But Mademoiselle Nanon wasn't forewarned.

BISCARROS

(entering)

Sir?

CANOLLES

My hat, my cane, my sword.

(to Castorin)

My letter?

CASTORIN

Here it is—oh, sir, my sides. I'll have to stay in bed for two weeks.

CANOLLES

Saddle the horses—we are leaving.

CASTORIN

What do you mean we're leaving?

CANOLLES

Let's go—hurry!

CASTORIN

But, sir—

(Canolles raps the table; frightened, Castorin escapes).

CANOLLES

(to Biscarros reentering)

This letter by one of your waiters to Mademoiselle Nanon de Lartigues, to her or to Mademoiselle Francinette, you understand.

BISCARROS

By God!

CANOLLES

And now, the Vicomte.

BISCARROS

What about the Vicomte?

CANOLLES

Yes, which way did he go? What road did he take?

BISCARROS

He went by way of the Paris road.

CANOLLES

This glove, it's indeed hers, right?

BISCARROS

Hers?

CANOLLES

Yes—his or hers—little matter! Oh, I will rejoin her, oh! I will kiss the hand that served as the mold for this glove.

(seizing Biscarros by the throat)

Biscarros—Biscarros, you are a wretch for not having told me that the Vicomte was a woman.

BISCARROS

Baron, baron—you are strangling me!

CANOLLES

(tossing him a purse)

Here—and shut up! I entrust you with this letter for Mademoiselle Francinette—my horse! My horse!

BISCARROS

Is it conceivable, Dear God!, that a mere glove can put a man in such a frenzy?

CURTAIN

ACT II

SCENE 3

A boudoir with a door at the back. A large window with a balcony.

NANON

(seated on the couch)

Well, Mademoiselle, what were those shouts we heard just now? Are you informed?

FRANCINETTE

Oh, Madame, it's poor Castorin who wanted to come in here through the little door on the meadow—and he's fallen, it would seem into an ambush.

NANON

In an ambush?

FRANCINETTE

Madame, I think that the Duke was informed that we expected Monsieur de Canolles this evening, and that he placed his men armed with muskets on the master's entrance—and some men with sticks at the servant's entrance.

NANON

Ah, my God—what are you telling me?

FRANCINETTE

Here, Madame, here—look in the moonlight.

NANON

Four armed men, preceded by a man in a cloak. The man in the cloak—it's the Duke.

FRANCINETTE

The Duke!

NANON

(looking at the table)

I am lost. These two place settings, these two chairs—the table covered—I will never have the time.

FRANCINETTE

Suppose I order Baptist not to open?

NANON

Not at all! On the contrary—go open yourself. It's the Duke that I am expecting, not Monsieur de Canolles.

(Francinette leaves. A dry rapping at the door.)

NANON

(alone)

This goblet by the window, it's the Duke's and in its place. This covering is in the drawer. Where is the Duke's table setting? Ah, here it is. Now, the wine, the wine he's used to drinking.

(taking a bottle of wine from an armoire and putting it on the table)

Come, come, Nanon, the rest is your business.

(The sound of a step on the stair can be heard—opening the door.)

But come, my Duke, come—ah, my dream did not deceive me, Dear Duke?

DUKE

One moment, Mademoiselle, one moment! And let's begin with an explanation if you please.

(looking around everywhere)

NANON

Now what's the matter with you, my dear Duke? Did you forget something the last time that you came that you are looking around now?

DUKE

Yes, I forgot to tell you I was not a fool, a Geronte like Monsieur Cyrano de Bergerac puts in his comedies.

NANON

I don't understand you, I beg you to explain yourself.

DUKE

Hum! Hum!

NANON

(with a curtsy)

I am awaiting the good pleasure of your Lordship.

DUKE

The good pleasure of my Lordship that you tell me why this supper?

NANON

Because, as I repeat to you, I had a dream which told me that although you left me yesterday, you would return today.

DUKE

And this charming negligee, Madame?

NANON

But it seems to me when I expect Milord, I wait for him dressed for battle.

DUKE

So, you were expecting me?

NANON

Ah, so that's it! Milord, God pardon me, but I think you'd like to search the closets. Would you be jealous, by chance?

DUKE

(taking off his cloak and sitting on the couch)

Me jealous? Oh, no, thank God! I am not so ridiculous. Old and rich, I know that I am born to be deceived. But I intend, at least, to test those who deceive me so as not to be their dupe.

NANON

And how will you test them? I am curious to know it.

DUKE

Oh—it won't be difficult. I am not dreaming. At my age, one no longer dreams—even awake—but one receives letters—read this one, it is interesting.

NANON

(takes the letter and reads it)

"Milord Duke is warned that, this evening a man who is familiar with Mademoiselle Nanon de Lartigues will be with her—and he will stay to supper and sleep over. So as not to leave the Duke in any uncertainty, one can tell him that this happy rival is named the Baron de Canolles."

(aside)

De Cauvignac's writing. Ah I was wise to be rid of him.

(to Duke)

Is it possible that a man of your genius, that a deep politician like you allows himself to be taken in by an anonymous letter. Here, there's your letter.

DUKE

Pardon me, but you haven't read the postscript.

NANON

The postscript?

DUKE

Yes, read.

NANON

(reading)

"I have in my hands the original of a letter from Mademoiselle Nanon de Lartigues to Monsieur de Canolles. I will give this letter in return for a blank pardon which the Duke will send me today at three in the afternoon at the ferry of Ison where I will await him."

(speaking to the Duke)

And you were imprudent enough to—

DUKE

Your writing is so precious to me, dear lady, that I didn't think I could ever pay too much for a letter of yours.

NANON

Then you have my letter?

DUKE

Here it is—oh—read it aloud.

NANON

(reading)

"I will dine at ten o'clock. Are you free? I am. In that case, be on time, my dear Canolles—and don't worry about our secret."

DUKE

Well, that's plain enough it seems to me.

NANON

(joyously)

Ah!

DUKE

Ah! You have a secret with Monsieur de Canolles?

NANON

Well, yes.

DUKE

You admit it?

NANON

Well, I must since nothing can hidden from you. Now, do you know who Monsieur de Canolles is?

DUKE

He's your lover, Madame.

NANON

You are mistaken, Duke—he is—my brother.

DUKE

Your brother? This requires an explanation.

NANON

And I am going to give it to you. At what period did my father die?

DUKE

Why—about fifteen months, ago more or less.

NANON

At what period did you sign the commission as Captain for Monsieur de Canolles.

DUKE

Around the same time.

NANON

Two weeks later, sir.

DUKE

Two weeks later? It's possible.

NANON

It's sad for me to reveal the shame of another woman, to reveal what is our secret, not yours, you understand! But your strange jealousy forces me, your cruel manners oblige me—I imitate you, Duke—I am wanting in generosity.

DUKE

Continue! Continue!

NANON

Well, my father was a lawyer who didn't lack a certain fame though he died without fortune. At twenty-eight my father was young, my father was handsome—he loved the mother of Monsieur de Canolles because she was noble and he was a commoner. Love took care of all that as often happens. And during the absence of Monsieur de Canolles on a voyage—you understand now—right?

DUKE

Yes—but, why did this great friendship for Monsieur de Canolles come to you so late?

NANON

Because only on the death of my father did I learn of the bond which unites us.

DUKE

Ah! Ah!

NANON

Twenty times I wanted to tell you this story, very sure you would do much for the man I call my brother. But he always held me back, always begged me to spare the reputation of his mother who is still living. I respected his scruples, since I understood them.

DUKE

Ah, truly.

NANON

And especially since he was refusing to make his fortune.

DUKE

He is a delicate soul.

NANON

And I who took an oath never to reveal this mystery to anyone in the world, misfortune to me for betraying the secrets of my brother.

DUKE

You say "Misfortune to me," Nanon; instead say, "Good fortune for us all." I intend to repair the times wasted, this dear Canolles. I don't know him; I wish to make his acquaintance.

NANON

Well, I will present him to you tomorrow.

DUKE

Tomorrow? Why not this evening?

NANON

What do you mean this evening?

DUKE

Yes, can't the boy come to dine with us? Wait, I am going this very moment to send someone to find him at the Golden Calf.

NANON

So he will know that concerning all my oaths, I told you everything?

DUKE

Never mind, I will be discreet.

NANON

Indeed, Duke, I am going to pick a quarrel with you.

DUKE

Why's that?

NANON

Because, before, you were more fond of a tete a tete. Look, believe me, it will be time to send to look for him tomorrow.

DUKE

We will see him after supper, darling. Francinette! Francinette!

NANON

What are you doing?

DUKE

(to Francinette as she enters)

Francinette, ask for orders from your mistress.

NANON

(sitting on the couch)

Give yours, Duke—aren't you at home?

DUKE

Go to the Golden Calf and tell Monsieur de Canolles that Mademoiselle Nanon de Lartigues is expecting him for supper.

NANON

(to Francinette who questions her with a glance)

Go! I hope that he will understand in a few words.

DUKE

(sitting near Nanon)

Do you know why I hope to see your brother this evening, darling?

NANON

I do not know—unless it may be to be sure that Monsieur de Canolles is indeed my brother.

DUKE

Do I doubt when you have said something, darling? No, it's that if it's agreeable to him and you as well, I would have a special mission to give him at court.

NANON

A mission?

DUKE

Yes, but it will separate you and—

NANON

Oh, don't worry, my dear Duke. What does a separation matter, since it will be profitable to him? Moreover, I will serve him ill since I see that you are still jealous, but far away you will make his way with your power. Exile him, expatriate him, if it's for his benefit, so long as the love of my dear Duke remains with me—which is all I require to make me happy.

DUKE

Well, it's done—we will send him to Paris—to the Court—we will make his fortune.

(a scratching at the door)

What is that?

FRANCINETTE

(entering)

Madame, the Baron de Canolles is no longer at the Golden Calf.

NANON

Ah!

DUKE

The Baron is no longer at the Golden Calf?

NANON

Ah. Surely you are mistaken.

FRANCINETTE

Madame, I repeat what Monsieur Biscarros just told me. He himself prepared his dinner.

NANON

(aside)

Ah, this dear Canolles must have figured out everything.

DUKE

Tell Master Biscarros to come in.

NANON

Let's see, miss, obey the Duke.

FRANCINETTE

Come in, Monsieur Biscarros, come in!

(Biscarros enters.)

NANON

(seated)

Sir, you had a young gentleman called Baron de Canolles with you this evening, right?

DUKE

(seated near the table)

Yes, what has become of him?

BISCARROS

The gentleman left.

NANON

Left?

DUKE

Indeed left? Truly left?

BISCARROS

Truly.

DUKE

And where did he go?

BISCARROS

That I cannot tell you, for I don't know.

DUKE

You know at least what route he took?

BISCARROS

The Paris road.

DUKE

And at what time did he take that route?

BISCARROS

Maybe a half hour—a little less.

NANON

What! He left without saying anything?

BISCARROS

Indeed, he charged me to take a letter to Mademoiselle Francinette.

DUKE

And why didn't you send her the letter, scoundrel?

BISCARROS

I did better, I brought it to her myself.

DUKE

Francinette! Francinette!

FRANCINETTE

Here.

DUKE

Why didn't you give your mistress the letter that Monsieur de Canolles sent for her.

FRANCINETTE

Milord!

BISCARROS

"Milord"—he's some prince in disguise.

NANON

I didn't ask her for it, that's why!

DUKE

You couldn't ask her for it since you were unaware that she had received it—let me have that letter.

FRANCINETTE

Here!

DUKE

(taking the letter)

Hum!

FRANCINETTE

(to Biscarros)

Imbecile!

DUKE

What is this scrawl?

NANON

Read it.

DUKE

"Dear Nanon, I am profiting from the leave Monsieur d'Épernon has accorded me and to distract me, I am going to use the time to gallop to Paris—till I see you again! I place my fortune in your hands."

But this Canolles is crazy.

NANON

(breathing)

Mad! Why? Don't you see what it's about?

DUKE

Not the faintest idea.

NANON

Well, Monsieur de Canolles is twenty-seven years old, he is young, he is handsome, he is carefree—to what folly do you think he gives his presence? To love—! He saw some pretty traveler at Monsieur Biscarros' inn and he's following her.

DUKE

In love? You think Canolles is in love?

NANON

Doubtless. Here, as Monsieur Biscarros, haven't I guessed right, Master Biscarros?

(Francinette signals Biscarros to say yes.)

BISCARROS

(aside)

I think the moment has come for me to repair my stupidity.

(aloud)

In fact, Madame may well be right.

NANON

You think so?

BISCARROS

The fact is you've opened my eyes.

NANON

Ah! Tell us about it, Master Biscarros. Let's see, tell us who
were the travelers who stopped at your inn tonight?

DUKE

Yes, tell us that.

BISCARROS

There were tourists.

NANON

(breathing)

Ah!

BISCARROS

Just a little gentleman, dark-skinned, delicate, plump—who didn't eat, who didn't drink, who was afraid to travel at night. A gentleman who was afraid, you understand?

DUKE

Ah! Ah! Ah! Yes, I understand.

NANON

Continue, it's charming! And doubtless this little gentleman expected Monsieur de Canolles?

BISCARROS

Not at all! He was waiting to dine with a large, heavily mustached gentleman. He was even a bit rough with Monsieur de Canolles—when Monsieur de Canolles wanted to dine with him—but he was not disconcerted by such a little thing, the brave gentleman. Ah, he's a daring companion, and my word after the big fellow left, he rushed after the small fellow who went the other way.

DUKE

Truly?

NANON

Oh! But what makes you think this little gentleman may be a woman, that Monsieur de Canolles may be amorous of this woman, and that he did not take the main road from boredom or capriciousness?

BISCARROS

I will tell you what makes me thank that.

DUKE

Yes, tell us my friend. Truly, you are very amusing.

BISCARROS

Sir, you are very kind. What made me think it—then—it's a glove.

NANON

Why a glove?

BISCARROS

I suspected nothing—I took the dark skinned little fellow for a man when Monsieur de Canolles called me in a fury. He was holding in his hand this little glove which he examined and was smiling, passionately.

NANON

A glove! A glove like this?

(giving him a glove)

BISCARROS

Not at all—a man's glove.

NANON

(taking it back)

A man's glove? You are mad!

BISCARROS

No, for this glove, belonged to the little gentleman, the pretty little dark-skinned fellow who didn't drink, who didn't eat, who was afraid—in this glove Madame's hand could hardly get in, although Madame has a pretty little hand.

NANON

Well, Duke, I hope you are sufficiently informed and that you know what you want to know.

FRANCINETTE

(low to Biscarros)

Oh—you wretch!

BISCARROS

(low to Francinette)

What do you mean, wretch?

FRANCINETTE

Yes, wretch!

BISCARROS

(aloud)

After all, Monsieur de Canolles left, it's true, but he might return at any moment.

DUKE

It's true—in his letter, he speaks only of taking a gallop. Go see, Master Biscarros if he's returned and bring him here.

BISCARROS

Milord.

(going to leave)

NANON

But you aren't thinking of it! And the supper, Duke? First of all, I am dying of hunger.

DUKE

That's true, stay Master Biscarros. Cortanvaux! Come here.

(Cortanvaux enters.)

DUKE

Run to Master Biscarros' inn and see if Monsieur de Canolles has not returned—and if he's not there—look around the neighborhood and inform yourself. I want to dine with this gentleman.

CORTANVAUX

It will be done, Milord.

(Cortanvaux exits.)

FRANCINETTE

(low to Biscarros)

You've just done some fine work!

BISCARROS

Me?

FRANCINETTE

Come on, let's go—and in the future try to keep your mouth shut!

BISCARROS

(leaving)

If I understood what was going on.

(Exit Biscarros and Francinette.)

NANON

What a misfortune that the stupidity of this crazy Canolles keeps him from the honor you were going to do him. If he had been here, his future would be assured. Wait—

DUKE

What?

NANON

You weren't going to send him to the Queen?

DUKE

Doubtless—but since he's not here—

NANON

Well, send someone after him and since he's on the way to Paris, the way he's taken is known—

DUKE

(rising)

You are quite right.

NANON

(rising)

Let me manage this and Monsieur de Canolles will have the order tomorrow morning—I will answer to you for it.

DUKE

Oh—the fine head of a diplomat. You will go far Nanon.

NANON

So long as I remain eternally at my education with such a fine master—that's as far as my ambition takes me.

DUKE

Hum!

NANON

What a delicious joke to play on us, huh? Here, let's not lose any time, look Duke, prepare your dispatch—I will prepare mine.

DUKE

Oh—mine is short.

NANON

And mine will not take long.

(sitting and writing at the table near the couch)

DUKE

(writing)

"Bordeaux! No!"

(he hides the letter)

NANON

(writing)

"My dear Baron, as you see the dispatch joined to this is for Her Majesty, the Queen, on your life—take it to her instantly—it's a question of well being of the Kingdom. Your good sister—Nanon."

DUKE

(writing)

"To Her Majesty, Queen Anne of Austria, Regent of France."

NANON

(writing)

"To Baron de Canolles on the road to Paris." Here, Duke—

DUKE

Here, darling.

CORTANVAUX

(entering)

Monsieur de Canolles.

NANON

Canolles!

DUKE

The Baron?

CORTANVAUX

I met him not a hundred feet from here.

NANON

(falling onto the couch)

He said I wouldn't avoid him.

(Cauvignac enters dressed splendidly.)

NANON

(noticing Cauvignac)

Him!

CAUVIGNAC

Eh! Doubtless me, dear little sister.

NANON

Cauvignac! Cauvignac!

CAUVIGNAC

(to Duke)

I beg your pardon, perhaps I am in the way?

DUKE

Be welcome, Monsieur de Canolles, your sister and I have been speaking of you for over an hour, and for an hour we've wanted you—

CAUVIGNAC

Ah! You want me—truly?

NANON

Yes, the Duke has had the goodness to ask that you be presented to him.

CAUVIGNAC

Sir, the fear of being a nuisance has prevented me from claiming this honor sooner.

DUKE

In fact, Baron, I admire your delicacy and I reproach you for it.

CAUVIGNAC

Reproach me for my delicacy—me, sir? Ah—you confuse me.

DUKE

Yes, for if your good sister hadn't cared for your interests—

CAUVIGNAC

Ah, my dear sister has taken care of my interests.

NANON

What is more natural than to take care of her brother's interests?

DUKE

And today even, to what do I owe the pleasure of seeing you?

CAUVIGNAC

Yes, to what do you owe the pleasure of seeing me—?

DUKE

Well, to chance—to pure chance which made you return.

CAUVIGNAC

(to Nanon)

Ah!

NANON

Yes, you had left, bad brother, and with no other warning than a short note which redoubled my anxiety.

DUKE

What do you want, dear Nanon, he must spend some time on love—

CAUVIGNAC

(to Nanon)

Oh! Oh! This is getting complicated—me—amorous?

NANON

Come, admit that you—bad boy!

CAUVIGNAC

Well, I won't deny it.

DUKE

Well, well, but let's dine. You well tell us of your loves as we dine. Francinette, a place setting for Monsieur de Canolles— can we put him to the account of the little gentleman.

NANON

Perfectly.

CAUVIGNAC

Pardon, what gentleman?

NANON

Of the little gentleman you met this evening.

CAUVIGNAC

Ah—my word, that's true—the little gentleman.

NANON

Ah! Ah!—you really met him?

CAUVIGNAC

The little gentleman? By God!

NANON

How was he? Look—tell us frankly.

CAUVIGNAC

My word, he was a charming little companion, dark, svelte, elegant, fifteen to sixteen years of age, still no mustaches, traveling with an old squire.

(aside)

Damn, I am giving them what I saw—so much the worse if it doesn't work.

NANON

That's him!

DUKE

That's him.

CAUVIGNAC

(aside)

Goodness, it is working.

DUKE

Are you still wearing the little pearl grey glove on your heart?

CAUVIGNAC

The little pearl gray glove?

DUKE

Yes, the one you kissed and sniffed so passionately which made you suspect the ruse, the metamorphosis.

CAUVIGNAC

Ah! So it was a woman? Well, I suspected it, word of honor.

DUKE

Come, come, all this is very fine and since the affairs of the King do not suffer by it—

CAUVIGNAC

The affairs of the King suffer for it? Never! The affairs of the King are sacred.

DUKE

They can count on your devotion, Baron?

CAUVIGNAC

To the King? Why, for the King, I will be drawn and quartered.

NANON

And it's quite simple—aren't you captain in the service of His Majesty, thanks to the bounty of the Duke?

CAUVIGNAC

(rising and putting his hand on his heart)

And I will never forget it!

DUKE

We will do better, Baron, we will do better in the future. While waiting your sister will in a few words make you au-courant of what we have already done.

CAUVIGNAC

(aside)

That wouldn't be bad.

DUKE

She has a letter to confide to you on my behalf. Perhaps your fortune is in the message that I am giving you—take the advice of your sister, young man, take her advice—she's got a good head—a distinguished wit, a generous heart. Love your sister, Baron, and you will be in my good graces.

CAUVIGNAC

Milord, my sister knows to what degree I love her—I desire nothing more than to see her happy, powerful and rich—especially rich.

(Nanon rises.)

DUKE

This warmth please me—

(rising)

Stay with Nanon while I go to occupy myself with a certain clown.

CAUVIGNAC

(at the table)

Huh?

DUKE

By the way, Baron, perhaps you could give me some information about this bandit?

CAUVIGNAC

I? Willingly! Only I need to know of which bandit you speak. There are so many of all types in these times.

DUKE

You are right—but this one is one of the most impudent that I have ever met.

CAUVIGNAC

Ah, truly?

DUKE

Imagine that this wretch, in exchange for a letter your sister wrote you yesterday, and which he obtained through an infamous act of violence, extorted from me a blank pardon. I wanted to ask you if you have some idea who played the role of informer?.

CAUVIGNAC

In truth, no.

DUKE

No matter—he will be lucky if his pardon doesn't get him hanged.

CAUVIGNAC

You kept his description?

DUKE

No—but on his pardon I placed a mark.

NANON

A mark?

CAUVIGNAC

A mark? And he didn't notice it, the imbecile?

DUKE

Invisible—my dear—invisible to all—but visible to me with the aid of a chemical process.

CAUVIGNAC

Ah, ah—yes—wait, wait, wait, but that's the most ingenious thing, what you did there, Milord. Only you must take care he doesn't suspect the trick.

DUKE

Oh—there's no danger of that; which of you would want to tell him?

CAUVIGNAC

In fact, it won't be Nanon and it won't be me.

DUKE

Nor I.

CAUVIGNAC

Nor you! So you're right, Milord—you cannot fail one day to identify this man—

DUKE

Then I will be even with him, waiting to exchange his pardon, he will have received what he desires—then I will hang him.

CAUVIGNAC

Amen!

DUKE

Now, since you cannot give me any information about this comedian—

CAUVIGNAC

No, Milord, I cannot—

DUKE

Well, I am going to leave you with your sister. Nanon, give this boy precise instructions, and don't let him waste any time.

NANON

Rest assured, Milord.

DUKE

So—to both of you.

(Nanon escorts the Duke to the door.)

CAUVIGNAC

The Devil! The worthy lord did well to warn me. But what will I do with the blank pardon? Damn, what one does with a letter, I will discount it. Madame de Condé, exactly, wrote to Nanon—it's business to do at Chantilly.

NANON

Now, sir, to the two of us, as Monsieur d'Épernon just said.

CAUVIGNAC

Yes, darling little sister—for I come to have a discussion with you.

(He sits on the couch.)

NANON

(with rage)

Sir, tell me how a brother, overwhelmed with my bounties, has coldly conceived the project of destroying his sister?

CAUVIGNAC

I, dear Nanon? Never! I would lose too much in ruining you.

NANON

Do you deny that this anonymous letter was in your handwriting?

CAUVIGNAC

No, since you recognized it.

NANON

So, you confess?

CAUVIGNAC

What have you against this letter? You find it poorly written perchance? That would irritate me with you, it would prove you have no taste for literature.

NANON

But what motive made you write this letter?

CAUVIGNAC

What motive? Nanon—it's a little act of revenge.

NANON

An act of revenge against me, wretch! But what wrong have I done for the idea of avenging yourself on me to come to your mind?

CAUVIGNAC

What have you done? Ah, Nanon, put yourself in my place. I left Paris because I had too many enemies. That's the misfortune of a political man. I came to you; I implored you—you remember that? You received three letters—you aren't telling me you don't recognize my writing—it's exactly the same as the anonymous letter—anyway the letters were signed. I wrote you 3 letters to ask you for a wretched hundred pistoles, 100 pistoles—from you who have millions.

(rising)

Well, my sister repulsed me. I came to my sister's place, my sister shows me the door, naturally I inform myself. Perhaps she is in distress—it's the moment to prove to her that her benefits have not fallen on ungrateful territory. Perhaps she is no longer free—in that case, she's pardonable, for you see my heart searched for excuses for you and it's then that I learned my sister is free, happy, right, very rich, and that a Baron de Canolles, a stranger is usurping my privileges and has made himself protector in my place. Then, jealousy turned my head.

NANON

Say cupidity, sir! What did it matter to you if I had or did not have friendly relations with Monsieur de Canolles?

CAUVIGNAC

To me? Fine. I wouldn't have even been uneasy if you had continued to have financial relations with me, ingrate!

NANON

What do you mean, ingrate?

CAUVIGNAC

Yes, ingrate. Do you deny that I had just extricated you from the worst position a woman can find herself in? I profited from this to the extent there remained some money to allow me to dress to the nines—so you wouldn't have cause to be ashamed of me. Look at me a bit—it seems to me. I have a nice look this way, eh?

NANON

Hum!

CAUVIGNAC

What do you mean, "hum"? Dear friend, you are difficult—but never mind. I came here and I understood from the first word, from the first glance that you were floundering in a really false fraternity. I took on my count the adventure of the dark skinned little gentleman; I admitted to have kissed a glove at some risk. Yet, since then, thanks to good old Cauvignac your family novel became a history. My presence saved everything. Your brother is no longer a lie. You are free like the wind, you will sleep soundly—thanks to good old Cauvignac. As for me, I am installing myself right here—Monsieur d'Épernon is making me a colonel. In place of a squad of five men, I have a regiment of two thousand; I renew the labors of Hercules! I'll be named Duke and Peer; Madame d'Épernon dies and Monsieur d'Épernon marries you.

NANON

Quit joking, sir.

CAUVIGNAC

Oh—I am not joking.

NANON

Two things.

CAUVIGNAC

Which are? Speak.

NANON

Prima, you are going to return the blank pardon to the Duke—without that you will be hanged.

CAUVIGNAC

Prima hanged? And second?

NANON

Second: You are going to leave here instantly.

CAUVIGNAC

Two replies, dear lady, Prima—the blank pardon being my property, I am keeping it. Seconda—You cannot prevent me from being hanged if it is my good pleasure.

NANON

Oh! It's not just yours.

CAUVIGNAC

Thanks! But it won't happen, rest assured. As for my leaving, in your desire to be rid of me, you forget one thing.

NANON

Which is?

CAUVIGNAC

It's that if I retire, I cannot complete this important mission which the Duke spoke to me of just now—and which will make my fortune.

NANON

But wretch, you know quite well that this mission is not intended for you—it is intended for Monsieur de Canolles.

CAUVIGNAC

Well, but am I not called Monsieur de Canolles? Also, consider dear sister, it's not for you to impose conditions on me—it's for me to impose conditions on you.

NANON

Let's see—what are they?

CAUVIGNAC

First and most important of all—general amnesty.

NANON

And then?

CAUVIGNAC

Then pay our reckoning.

NANON

I must owe you something, it seems.

CAUVIGNAC

You owe me the 100 pistoles that I asked you for and which you
inhumanly refused me.

NANON

That's all right—the amnesty is granted.

CAUVIGNAC

Then your hand, dear little sister.

(kissing her hand)

Ah—and the hundred pistoles.

NANON

(going to a desk)

Here are two hundred.

CAUVIGNAC

Two hundred! Good—finally I recognize my sister.

NANON

But on one condition.

CAUVIGNAC

Which is?

NANON

That you repair the harm you have done.

CAUVIGNAC

I only came for that—what is to be done? Let's see—?

NANON

Take horse and rush toward Paris until you meet Monsieur de
Canolles.

CAUVIGNAC

What must I tell him?

NANON

You will deliver this order to him. But how can I be sure you will complete my commission—? If there were something sacred to you, I would insist on an oath.

CAUVIGNAC

There's a better way!

NANON

Which is?

CAUVIGNAC

Promise me 200 pistoles, once the commission is completed.

NANON

That's agreed.

CAUVIGNAC

Well, look—I don't ask you for an oath. Your word suffices me. So, it's agreed, two hundred pistoles to the person who delivers Monsieur de Canolles' receipt.

NANON

(joyously)

You speak of—by chance, do you plan not to return?

CAUVIGNAC

Who knows? My own business calls me to the neighborhood of Paris.

NANON

(breathing)

Ah!

CAUVIGNAC

Ah! There's an "ah" which is not only me—but never mind—no rancor, dear sister.

NANON

(bringing him his cape and putting it on his shoulders)

No rancor, but to horse.

CAUVIGNAC

In a moment—give me time to drink a parting cup.

(drinking)

To the health of M. d'Épernon—he's a brave man.

CURTAIN

ACT II

SCENE 4

A bedroom in a hostel of the town of Jaulnay—door open to the left, door at the rear. An alcove for two beds. A window to the right.

CASTORIN

(sleeping on some chairs)

It's astonishing! It seems to me I'm still on horseback and that motion—oh—the sun's nice when one can sleep. Ah, the Baron does well not to get here for two hours. I will already have taken a nap.

HOST

(below)

This way, sir, there.

CASTORIN

Huh? What's that? Decidedly, no bed.

HOST

(coming in the left side door)

This way, sir, this way—here's the man you are looking for, I think.

CANOLLES

What—the clown is sleeping—without my permission? Go quickly, my horse needs water.

HOST

I am going.

(Exit Host.)

CANOLLES

Come on, come on, Castorin, to horse.

CASTORIN

(rocking on the chair)

But I am on horseback, sir.

CANOLLES

Look, wake up and answer, scoundrel.

CASTORIN

(stops rocking)

Oh!

CANOLLES

I am going to cut your ear off, that will wake you up.

CASTORIN

I am awake, sir. Now—where are we?

CANOLLES

In the Inn at Jaulnay, clown, where I ordered you to precede me.

CASTORIN

Oh, it's true—and I preceded you in such a way that my horse fell dead as he arrived in the courtyard. Poor animal! Well, I am sure he was less fatigued than I.

CANOLLES

Imbecile! Look, are you sure that the Vicomte hasn't passed this village?

CASTORIN

By God! Thanks to the short cut you made me take, I have more than an hour on him.

CANOLLES

And, according to my order, you rented the rooms of this inn?

CASTORIN

All—you have eight. Oh—you'll have a nice sleep tonight.

CANOLLES

And are you sure that the Vicomte didn't go to another inn than ours?

CASTORIN

Oh, as to that, I am sure of it, for there's only one in the village.

CANOLLES

The innkeeper didn't make any trouble?

CASTORIN

To rent his eight rooms? On the contrary only he doesn't understand how a master would need eight rooms—but I paid in advance and he understood.

CANOLLES

Very well—it looks like you wish to sleep?

CASTORIN

It looks that way, yes, sir.

CANOLLES

Well—in these eight rooms, is there one which pleases you?

CASTORIN

They all please me—only especially number seven, which is all gold.

CANOLLES

Take number seven.

CASTORIN

For me?

CANOLLES

For you! And I order you to sleep for twelve hours.

CASTORIN

Monsieur will be obeyed.

(Goes to leave.)

CANOLLES

Twelve hours, you understand—without stirring no matter what noise you hear in the house.

CASTORIN

Ah, sir, you can fire a cannon—it's all the same to me.

CANOLLES

That' fine! Send the innkeeper to me, and be gone.

(Exit Castorin.)

CANOLLES

(alone)

I has indeed thought to catch my little Vicomte on the big highway, to renew conversation with him—to share his dinner, his supper—but he's tricky, the little kid. He played me a trick and escaped me a second time. What's really frightful is not knowing for sure if I'm chasing a he or a she. If he is a man, such a blunder would be enough to die of. Ah, Canolles, you are made foolish by doubt as Castorin is by sleep. Anyway, in an hour, I'll resolve this doubt. While waiting, let's examine the room. An open door which gives on another room—an alcove with two beds. Good—let's place the quartermaster here.

(He rings.)

INNKEEPER

(entering from the rear)

You called me, sir?

CANOLLES

Yes—-what time do you usually close your door?

INNKEEPER

At eleven o'clock, sir, but as I am expecting no one, seeing that you've rented the whole place—I will close whenever you wish.

CANOLLES

Well, quite the contrary. I would like your doors to remain open.

INNKEEPER

But sir, I'm not longer expecting anyone.

CANOLLES

That's possible—but I am expecting someone.

INNKEEPER

Ah!

(looking through the window)

Would it be the people who have just arrived?

CANOLLES

Who are these people?

INNKEEPER

A small young man of sixteen to eighteen years and an old squire.

CANOLLES

That's it.

INNKEEPER

I will go tell them that you are waiting for them.

CANOLLES

Hush, on the contrary. Not a word.

INNKEEPER

Then I am going to tell them there's no room for them.

CANOLLES

You are going to lodge them.

INNKEEPER

Where's that?

CANOLLES

In this room.

INNKEEPER

Ah, I understand! You will take #7.

CANOLLES

No, since my servant has taken it.

INNKEEPER

But—

CANOLLES

My dear fellow, you've been paid, right?

INNKEEPER

Yes, sir.

CANOLLES

Well then, what's bothering you?

INNKEEPER

But if they pay me?

CANOLLES

You will be paid twice.

INNKEEPER

That's all?

CANOLLES

Yes! Only—

INNKEEPER

Ah!

CANOLLES

After the strangers enter—shut your doors.

(voices in the wings)

Hurry! I believe the travelers are impatient.

INNKEEPER

I am off.

CANOLLES

Wait—another 300 pistoles. By the way—this room has another door giving on the corridor.

INNKEEPER

Parallel to this here, yes, sir.

(Noise outside.)

CANOLLES

Go down quickly, they are calling you.

(Innkeeper leaves.)

CANOLLES

I believe he's angry—word of a gentleman—it's the voice of a Vicomte—he's climbing the stairs—he approaches—when he walks—it's the step of a lady.

(He leaves by the open door.)

(Enter the Vicomtess, Pompey, and the Innkeeper with a light.)

THE VICOMTESS

(in the wings)

Well—are we there yet?

INNKEEPER

(entering)

This way, sir, this way.

THE VICOMTESS

This is what you have to offer me?

INNKEEPER

Oh—the room is good—it will be for you—the one on the side, a little less elegant will be for your squire.

THE VICOMTESS

An open doorway? Oh! No thanks!

INNKEEPER

Damn—it's take it or leave it, gentlemen.

THE VICOMTESS

Leave it then.

INNKEEPER

As you like it.

POMPEY

Vicomte, I will put my cloak over the opening.

THE VICOMTESS

No—and you don't have an office, a garret, a—?

INNKEEPER

I have a little loft at the end of the hall.

THE VICOMTESS

Oh—I prefer that. Excuse me, my brave Pompey—you know I cannot stand anyone around me when I sleep.

INNKEEPER

You must decide quickly sir, because from one moment to the next someone may arrive—the room was occupied.

THE VICOMTESS

What—it was occupied?

INNKEEPER

Yes, by a gentleman—but he left saying he would sleep with a friend he has in the neighborhood.

THE VICOMTESS

But if he returns?

INNKEEPER

Oh—at eleven o'clock—it's not likely.

THE VICOMTESS

That's fine, I will take your room.

POMPEY

Bah—in war it's like war—Vicomte, sir, and when one has traveled sixteen leagues—

THE VICOMTESS

You are tired, my brave Pompey?

POMPEY

Me? Never!

(sits down)

INNKEEPER

You have need of anything?

THE VICOMTESS

Not a thing, no.

INNKEEPER

(at the door)

Of nothing?

THE VICOMTESS

No, of nothing.

(Innkeeper leaves.)

THE VICOMTESS

Pompey, my valise.

POMPEY

Here it is.

THE VICOMTESS

My necessaries! Fine, that's it. Wait.

POMPEY

What?

THE VICOMTESS

I want to inspect this room.

(taking a torch)

Oh—how dark it is.

POMPEY

Wait while I go light it up.

(entering)

Ah! Ah! It has a door.

THE VICOMTESS

A door?

POMPEY

Yes—giving on the corridor.

THE VICOMTESS

But then, I am no longer by myself.

POMPEY

Ah—yes—it shuts from within.

THE VICOMTESS

Lock it with the key and put the bolts in if there are any.

POMPEY

(pushing the bolts home)

There are some.

THE VICOMTESS

And this here.

POMPEY

(entering)

At the moment, the other door is shut and there's no one in this room.

THE VICOMTESS

It's also shut—no, check the window.

(shuts the door and bolts it)

POMPEY

Do you think that behind these curtains?

(he advances, the curtain rustles, he stops)

THE VICOMTESS

Good—shut the counterpane.

POMPEY

With a bar?

THE VICOMTESS

An iron bar?

POMPEY

Yes.

THE VICOMTESS

Fine—now go, Pompey, go! And tomorrow at day break.

POMPEY

(turning)

Do you want me to leave you my musket?

THE VICOMTESS

But do you think I'm dying of fear, Pompey? Go and take your musket with you.

(He leaves by the right; the Vicomtess goes to shut the door behind him.)

THE VICOMTESS

Truly, the Princess will never know what it has cost me to run these roads. Oh—what do I hear? Nothing. Probably the street door closing. Decidedly, heaven didn't destine me to become a fearless chief. Come on, everything's all right.

(putting her hat on a chair)

Where are my necessaries? I'm always afraid my hairs will fall out from my wig. Yesterday, Monsieur de Canolles watched my wig very carefully.

CANOLLES

(on the stairs)

That's fine! That's fine!

THE VICOMTESS

Huh! It's like having called on a spirit, it seemed to me that that voice—ah! But—they're coming upstairs—they're in the corridor—they're stopping at my door—they're putting a key in the lock—who is that? Who is there?

CANOLLES

(from the other side of the door)

I am asking who is there.

THE VICOMTESS

What, you?

CANOLLES

Without a doubt, me. What the devil! I have the right to ask who is in my room.

THE VICOMTESS

In your room? Oh, my God! It's doubtless the gentleman who ought not to return and who has returned. Sir, what do you want?

CANOLLES

It's very simple, I retained a room I wish to occupy it. Didn't the innkeeper tell you that this room was occupied by a gentleman who went to dine with one of his friends?

THE VICOMTESS

Yes, sir, it's true, but he said that in all probability, the gentleman would not return.

CANOLLES

The innkeeper was mistaken and the gentleman has returned.

(after a pause)

Well?

THE VICOMTESS

What, sir?

CANOLLES

I am waiting for you to have the goodness to open the door for me—unless you prefer me to smash it in?

THE VICOMTESS

Not at all, sir—I am opening—I am opening.

CANOLLES

(entering)

Truly—nice manners.

THE VICOMTESS

Monsieur de Canolles.

CANOLLES

The Vicomte—ah—so that's how you take my lodging? Good evening, Vicomte—how are you?

THE VICOMTESS

Baron—I am in despair.

(arranging her necessaries)

CANOLLES

God pardon me, he's already installed. Well—what are you doing there?

THE VICOMTESS

I am putting my things away—and I am going to call the Innkeeper.

CANOLLES

To do what?

THE VICOMTESS

But I don't wish you to sleep outside and since I came very late, I give up the place.

CANOLLES

But where will you go? There's no other Inn in Jaulnay.

THE VICOMTESS

I will go—I don't know where but I will go there.

CANOLLES

No, no, you are at home here—stay here—you are delicate, you are falling down from fatigue—go to bed peacefully and sleep—I will go find fortune elsewhere—the devil's in it if I cannot find some corner in this house!

THE VICOMTESS

Ah—sir, you are very obliging. Yes, I am delicate, yes I am tired, I will stay.

CANOLLES

And you are doing right.

THE VICOMTESS

Thanks! Thanks!

CANOLLES

Good night, Vicomte.

THE VICOMTESS

Good night.

CANOLLES

(returning)

Ah, but what have you there? A room—an empty room—that'll do for me.

THE VICOMTESS

Oh, no, no, Pompey is sleeping there—he's asleep.

CANOLLES

Well—but he'll wake up and get up.

THE VICOMTESS

Oh! pardon, you will find me very uncivil but Pompey is old, Pompey is not a servant—he's a friend.

CANOLLES

Well, sleep peacefully, Pompey—I know where to find a bed.

THE VICOMTESS

Oh—so much the better.

CANOLLES

Sleep soundly.

THE VICOMTESS

I'll answer for that.

CANOLLES

A handshake, Vicomte?

THE VICOMTESS

Very willingly.

(Canolles exits.)

THE VICOMTESS

Oh, but this young man is my evil genius, he makes me tremble, he makes me die. Poor boy—on the contrary—he is charming, clever, easy to get on with. Still, this room, the excuse was impertinent enough—come on, I'll hear no more of it—he's found fortune elsewhere as he said. Again the danger passes.

(opening her vest)

Why should I be afraid? The Inn is very quiet, it seems to me, everyone is asleep. In a quarter of an hour, He will sleep like the others. I admit that I wouldn't be angry to do so as well.

(a rap on the door)

Ah! My God! What is this?

CANOLLES

(outside)

Vicomte! Vicomte!

THE VICOMTESS

Again—Baron—what's wrong?

CANOLLES

Open up, open up—it's very serious.

THE VICOMTESS

(opening)

Speak quickly—come on!

CANOLLES

Ah! You are still nearly dressed—so much the better.

THE VICOMTESS

What does this agitation mean?

CANOLLES

Sit down.

(giving her a chair)

THE VICOMTESS

No, no—it's not necessary.

CANOLLES

Oh—it is—it's worth the trouble.

THE VICOMTESS

Truly!

(She sits.)

CANOLLES

I must tell you that the room where I had my heart set on—room #7 is occupied by two Swiss officers.

THE VICOMTESS

Ah.

CANOLLES

Yes—I asked them for their hospitality. I didn't wish to disturb you—you seem to me to be greatly in need of sleep.

THE VICOMTESS

It's true, I am very tired.

CANOLLES

Do you know what they responded, Vicomte? I was truly exasperated even more. No, it's an injury which cannot remain unpunished!

(rising)

Vicomte, do me the pleasure of taking your sword.

THE VICOMTESS

My sword! And to do what?

CANOLLES

Eh! By God! To come with me to rouse these clowns and invite them to go down to the garden. It's devilishly dark, but there's a lantern in the courtyard—let's go, let's go, Vicomte, come on.

THE VICOMTESS

But—

CANOLLES

(passing him his sword)

You clearly understand that if these scoundrels learn there were two French gentlemen here and that they left without beating them up, the French nation has been dishonored.

THE VICOMTESS

Doubtless, but—

CANOLLES

You are looking for your sword—here it is.

THE VICOMTESS

No, I would like to make you understand.

CANOLLES

What?

THE VICOMTESS

So you are not offended, Baron?

CANOLLES

How's that?

THE VICOMTESS

These fellows were sleeping, and when one is in one's first sleep, sometimes you are in a—different mood—then they are Swiss, you said?

CANOLLES

Doubtless.

THE VICOMTESS

Well, perhaps they didn't understand our language.

CANOLLES

If I repeated to you what they said to me, you would see they understood French perfectly.

THE VICOMTESS

Look, Baron, put yourself in their place, people in bed, asleep— it seems to me they are very excusable.

CANOLLES

The fact is, you are French, you are my compatriot, you put me out the door just now—but you didn't say to me what they said.

THE VICOMTESS

Pardon, Baron.

CANOLLES

You think I am not offended?

THE VICOMTESS

Oh—not in the least.

CANOLLES

In a way that in my place you wouldn't feel your honor demanded reparation.

THE VICOMTESS

No, no, I swear to you.

CANOLLES

You are full of sense, word of honor! Ah! You are not a young man!

THE VICOMTESS

I am not a young man?

CANOLLES

Because you are a Nestor, a wise man. Well, I forebear.

THE VICOMTESS

Ah!

(relaxing and sitting down)

CANOLLES

How come, two French gentlemen will be left baffled by these two rogues? No, no, wait by God—I must chase these two rogues out of their room—it's necessary.

THE VICOMTESS

(rising)

Come, has that got you again?

CANOLLES

Doubtless, if I don't chase them out, where shall I sleep, do you suppose? If you don't come, I will go alone—I will kill at least one. I will have his bed.

THE VICOMTESS

But if one of them kills you—?

CANOLLES

Well, then, I've found my bed forever.

THE VICOMTESS

Oh, no, no—I don't want—I beg you, Baron, for my sake, I would never be consoled.

CANOLLES

Damn—what do you want me to do?

THE VICOMTESS

(pointing to the side room)

There's plenty of room in this chamber.

CANOLLES

Pompey's room?

THE VICOMTESS

Yes.

CANOLLES

Pompey—who is sleeping? No, don't disturb Pompey—a brave
old fellow; your friend? No, I prefer to disturb my Swiss.

THE VICOMTESS

Pompey is no longer there.

CANOLLES

He is not there? Where is he then?

THE VICOMTESS

Just now, I sent him to sleep at the end of the corridor.

CANOLLES

Poor Pompey—and why's that?

THE VICOMTESS

Well, he snored too much.

CANOLLES

Oh—I sleep like a bird.

THE VICOMTESS

Well, take this room—take it!

CANOLLES

Oh—thanks, Vicomte!

THE VICOMTESS

Yes, yes.

CANOLLES

This is a deed I won't forget.

THE VICOMTESS

Take it and go to sleep quickly.

CANOLLES

Oh! I ask nothing better. I am falling asleep.

THE VICOMTESS

Good night, then!

CANOLLES

Good night dear friend.

(returning)

I don't know why I've got the idea that you've just given me advice which has saved my life.

THE VICOMTESS

Oh!

CANOLLES

Perhaps these Swiss would have killed me.

THE VICOMTESS

Oh, that's very likely.

CANOLLES

On my word! I have to embrace you!

THE VICOMTESS

Oh! Quite unnecessary.

(she pushes him into the adjoining room)

CANOLLES

Would you like me to lend you Castorin to unlace your boots?

THE VICOMTESS

No, no, thanks!

(Shutting the door behind him.)

CANOLLES

(from the room)

Ah, but it's an oven compared to your room, give me a light at least.

THE VICOMTESS

(putting out the light)

Oh—too bad! I put it out and have no more myself.

(she stands on a chair and puts her cloak over the opening)

Oh! I would give the 20,000 pounds I am bringing to Madame de Condé for it to be tomorrow—today.

(noise from Canolles)

Ah, my God, he's going to break his legs on the furniture!—Good! No more sound—he's found his bed. Oh, tomorrow I will leave without any fuss. Instead of following the main road, I will take a short cut. Ah, yes, for goodness sake! Wretched wig! It grips my head like a vise.

Ah, I can breathe.

(she shakes her head, her hair falls loose. horrible noise)

What happening, my God?

CANOLLES

Oh! Vicomte! Oh! Vicomte.

THE VICOMTESS

What?

CANOLLES

Something new!

THE VICOMTESS

What's wrong?

CANOLLES

Open up so I can tell you.

THE VICOMTESS

Open for him? Yes!

(a window pane breaks)

Oh, my God!

CANOLLES

God! While you were searching for the key, I broke a pane of glass.

(putting his hand through the opening and opening the door)

THE VICOMTESS

(hiding)

Sir! Sir!

CANOLLES

Can you imagine, Vicomte, that in drawing the curtains—

(going to the bed, the Vicomtess is near the window)

What the devil—down came the top of the bed. Huh, what luck I wasn't in it. Right? Right?

THE VICOMTESS

Yes, yes—it is very fortunate!

(she escapes and hides behind the window curtains)

CANOLLES

Are we playing blind man's bluff?

(he knocks against a chair)

Well, break your neck then—I was covered with dust. I was swimming in it. Why the devil did you extinguish your light? Where are you? Let's see. Like the Orpheus of Virgil I only embrace the air.

THE VICOMTESS

My clothes, great God! My Clothes! Well—what are you doing over there.

CANOLLES

(sitting)

I am looking for a bed.

THE VICOMTESS

What bed?

CANOLLES

One of yours; you aren't going to sleep in two beds, I hope. Isn't there some way to get some light?

THE VICOMTESS

Yes, I am looking, I am looking.

CANOLLES

What are you looking for?

THE VICOMTESS

The handbell to summon Pompey.

(Canolles, grasping the handbell which he found by fumbling on the table.)

CANOLLES

The handbell is there—what do you want Pompey for? What's he to do?

THE VICOMTESS

I want—I want him to make a bed in our room.

CANOLLES

For whom?

THE VICOMTESS

For him.

(She goes to the alcove.)

CANOLLES

For whom? What are you saying, Vicomte? Lackey in our room?
Come on, you have the ways of a frightened girl. Fie! We are
big enough boys to protect ourselves—no—just give me a hand
and guide me towards my bed, which I cannot find—or better
relight the candle.

THE VICOMTESS

No! No! No!

CANOLLES

Ah, I think I am there.

THE VICOMTESS

Yes, yes—you are there.

CANOLLES

Which of the two is mine?

THE VICOMTESS

The one you prefer.

(She runs into the alcove to get her vest back.)

CANOLLES

What are you doing?

THE VICOMTESS

No, I am not going to bed—I will spend the night in a chair.

CANOLLES

(returning)

Ah, for goodness sake—what I never put up with is childish-
ness—come, Vicomte, come.

(He opens the window shutter. Light spreads through the room.
Canolles advances, arms extended, toward the Vicomtess.)

THE VICOMTESS

Baron, don't come any closer, I beg you—not a step if you are
a gentleman.

(on her knees)

Mercy! Mercy!

CANOLLES

You—at my feet! Oh!

(He extends his arms.)

THE VICOMTESS

On your Mother's honor!

CAUVIGNAC

(in the street)

Monsieur de Canolles! Monsieur de Canolles!

THE VICOMTESS

I am saved!

CANOLLES

My name?

THE VICOMTESS

They are calling you, sir.

CANOLLES

By God! I hear it indeed.

CASTORIN

Monsieur de Canolles! Monsieur de Canolles!

(at the door)

CANOLLES

(opening the window)

Bawler!

CAUVIGNAC

Government courier.

CANOLLES

On whose behalf?

CAUVIGNAC

From the Duke d'Épernon—Open!

CASTORIN

From the Duke d'Épernon—Open!

THE VICOMTESS

From the Duke d'Épernon—Open!

(Canolles opens. They bring in some lights.)

CANOLLES

On behalf of the Duke d'Épernon? And what's he want of me—the Brute?

(takes him by the ear and pushes him across the room)

CAUVIGNAC

(entering)

Service of the King.

CANOLLES

Oh! Damn! There is a shame.

CAUVIGNAC

Plague! How you do travel, Baron! I thought I'd never overtake you—and now I've killed two horses.

CANOLLES

Your name, sir?

CAUVIGNAC

Oh—when I tell you name, it will not mean much to you—what matters to you is to know where I am coming from, and this letter will tell you that.

CANOLLES

(reading)

"My dear Baron, as you see, the dispatch attached is for Her Majesty, the Queen—on your life, bear it. This very moment— it deals with the well being of the kingdom—Nanon." Ah! It seems she got out her scrape by passing me for her brother— The letter for Her Majesty, sir?

CAUVIGNAC

Here it is. Milord, the Duke d'Épernon instructed me to tell you that Her Majesty is at Nantes.

CANOLLES

That's fine.

CAUVIGNAC

You've seen that the dispatch is urgent?

CANOLLES

I will leave in a moment, sir.

CAUVIGNAC

Now, please sign a receipt for me, the letter being important.

CANOLLES

(signing)

Here!

CAUVIGNAC

Baron, this signature will bring me two hundred pistoles—I wish that you will receive as much. You have nothing particular to say to Mademoiselle de Lartigues?

CANOLLES

Tell her that her brother appreciates the feeling which made her act, and is very obliged to her.

CAUVIGNAC

(bowing to Canolles and then the Vicomtess)

It appears I arrived just in time.

(He leaves.)

CANOLLES

Castorin, saddle the horses.

CASTORIN

(leaving)

Ah, if I had known, I would have remained in #7!

(Castorin exits.)

CANOLLES

(to the Countess who has put on her vest and wig)

Be content, Madame, you are going to be rid of me, I am leaving.

THE VICOMTESS

And when will that be?

CANOLLES

This very instant.

THE VICOMTESS

Goodbye, Sir!

CANOLLES

So—we are separated—perhaps forever!

THE VICOMTESS

Who knows?

CANOLLES

Promise one thing to a man who will eternally keep your memory.

THE VICOMTESS

What?

CANOLLES

That you will think of him sometimes.

THE VICOMTESS

I promise you!

CANOLLES

Without anger.

THE VICOMTESS

Yes.

CANOLLES

A proof—your hand.

(she gives him her hand which he carries to his lips)

Goodbye, Madame, goodbye—! Oh! Remember that you have

promised not to forget me.

THE VICOMTESS

Alas!

CURTAIN

ACT III
SCENE 5

Château Chantilly—the bedchamber of Madame de Condé.

DOWAGER

We failed, my daughter, we failed and we were humiliated.

MME DE TOURVILLE

You must pay a bit for a great deal of glory—there's no victory without combat.

PRINCESS

And if we fail, and if we are defeated—we will take vengeance.

DOWAGER

And on whom? On God? For God alone will have conquered the Prince. It's not an easy thing, especially by force, to open the door of the prisons of Vincennes.

MME DE TOURVILLE

Monsieur de Tourville, my husband, in his capacity as Master of Camp of the King's armies, had made while living and from the time that the Grand Prior was imprisoned, a plan to take Vincennes—he spoke often of it to me—I remembered it and I can communicate it to you.

DOWAGER

Thanks, my dear Madame de Tourville, but having on our side Monsieur de Turenne, Monsieur de Bouillon and Monsieur de la Rochefoucauld, I hope that between the three, they will find some way to extract my poor son from captivity.

PRINCESS

Oh—Monsieur de la Rochefoucauld, Monsieur Bouillon, and Monsieur de Turenne forget us. Claire herself has not arrived.

DOWAGER

My child, some obstacle must have stopped Madame de Cambes, for you know her devotion to our house is unalterable.

PRINCESS

While waiting, she hasn't arrived.

DOWAGER

Madame de Cambes must have been obliged to make some detours. The roads from Bordeaux, which they suspect us of wishing to retire to, are guarded by the army of Monsieur Saint-Aignan, and as Madame de Cambes is coming from Bordeaux—

MME DE TOURVILLE

At least she could write.

DOWAGER

Ah, dear Tourville, for a strategist of your ability! To write, to confide to paper the adhesion of a city like Bordeaux to the party of the princes would be very imprudent, you must agree.

MME DE TOURVILLE

One of three plans I had the honor to place before Your Highness had as its object the raising of Guyanne, and if it had been adopted—

PRINCESS

Fine! Fine! Dear Tourville, we will return to it if necessary—but while waiting, I am siding with my mother's opinion and begin to believe that Claire must have suffered some disgrace—otherwise, she should already be here. Perhaps her tenants failed in their word to her.

MME DE TOURVILLE

And all that, when one thinks that, if Monsieur Lenet, Monsieur Pierre Lenet, this opinionated councilor that you obstinately protect and is good only to oppose all our projects, when one thinks, I say, if Monsieur Lenet had not rejected my second plan—we would now have Bordeaux under siege and Bordeaux would have capitulated—!

LENET

(entering)

I prefer, saving the opinions of Their Highnesses, that Bordeaux join us willingly. A city which capitulates gives in to force and undertakes nothing. A city which willingly joins us thereby compromises itself and is forced to follow to the very end the fortunes of those it has willingly joined.

PRINCESS

Oh—it's useless to talk, my dear Lenet, everything is going from bad to worse and I much prefer a good courier to all these maxims.

LENET

Your Highness will be very satisfied for she will receive three today.

THE THREE WOMEN

What three?

LENET

Yes, Madame, the first was seen on the road from Bordeaux. The second comes from Stanay and the third is coming from La Rochefoucauld.

DOWAGER and PRINCESS

Oh!

MME DE TOURVILLE

It seems to me, my dear Monsieur Lenet, that a clever magician like you ought not to stay in such a vain condition and after having announced to us the coming of the couriers, he must also tell us the content of the dispatches.

LENET

My science doesn't go as far as you think. Madame—I am born to be a faithful servant. I announce, I do not foretell.

AN USHER

(entering)

A cavalier coming in all haste from Bordeaux claims the honor of being introduced to Her Highness.

LENET

First courier, Madame.

PRINCESS

You are a sorcerer, my dear Lenet, let him enter.

(Exit usher who returns with the Vicomtess.)

THE VICOMTESS

Madame!

PRINCESS

Claire! My dear Claire! In disguise.

THE VICOMTESS

Yes, Madame, and who begs you to accept her respectful homage. But my God, they told me that Your Highness fell from a horse and broke her leg.

PRINCESS

Hush! They say that, but reassure yourself, dear Vicomtess, it is nothing. It is only for our enemies that I broke my leg. Mazarin must believe me unable to move so he won't suspect I intend to flee.

THE VICOMTESS

Ah! Your Highness reassures me—

(starts to kneel)

Your Highness will permit—

PRINCESS

In my arms, dear Vicomtess, in my arms—

(embracing her)

And now, speak, speak quickly.

DOWAGER

Oh, yes, speak quickly, dear Vicomtess—have you seen Richon?

THE VICOMTESS

Yes, he charged me with a mission for Her Highness.

PRINCESS

Good or bad?

THE VICOMTESS

I don't know—it's only two words.

PRINCESS

Which are—I am dying of impatience.

THE VICOMTESS

"Bordeaux—yes!"

PRINCESS

Oh, bravo! Dear Claire, what luck—what a triumph! Come, Lenet, do you know what news this dear Vicomtess brings us?

LENET

Bordeaux, yes. Right?

PRINCESS

And you are right, Pierre, my good Pierre, always right. Still we owe this to this brave Richon. What shall we do for him?

DOWAGER

We must give him some important position—did he tell you what he wanted?

THE VICOMTESS

Yes, he wanted you to obtain for him the command of a stronghold like Varyres or Fort St. Georges.

PRINCESS

Alas, we are very bad in the court to recommend someone—

THE VICOMTESS

We have a blank order which we can use as a commission for Richon.

LENET

It's done, Madame.

PRINCESS

What do you mean it's done?

LENET

A letter has been sent by me to Mademoiselle de Lartigues— they say that this woman sells everything to any buyer—and as she controls the signature of Monsieur d'Épernon.

DOWAGER

Truly, my dear Lenet, you are a miraculous man! Only suppose Mademoiselle de Lartigues places a rather high price on a blank order from the Duke—I don't see how can we do much in our situation.

LENET

(to Vicomtess)

Here's the moment, Madame, to prove to Their Highnesses that we have thought of everything.

PRINCESS

What do you mean to say, Lenet?

THE VICOMTESS

That I am very happy to offer you a poor sum of 20,000 pounds, as miserable as it is, I have been able to obtain from my tenants.

PRINCESS

20,000 pounds?

DOWAGER

But that's a fortune in these times. And this purse, dear Vicomtess?

THE VICOMTESS

Is in your room, Madame, if Pompey has followed the orders I gave him.

PRINCESS

What is that noise?

LENET

Probably our second courier.

PRINCESS

And where is this one coming from?

LENET

Probably from Monsieur de la Rochefoucauld, whose father just died at Verticuil.

AN USHER

(entering)

An envoy of Madame de la Rochefoucauld solicits the honor of presenting homage to Their Highnesses.

PRINCESS

Have him come in.

THE VICOMTESS

Do you permit me to abandon this costume?

PRINCESS

Go—and return quickly.

(The Vicomtess exits.)

USHER

(announcing)

Monsieur de Tourville.

(La Rochefoucauld enters.)

PRINCESS

You come on behalf of Monsieur de la Rochefoucauld, sir? What news do you bring? But it's Monsieur de la Rochefoucauld himself.

LA ROCHEFOUCAULD

Yes, Madame, I have used the pretext of my father's funeral to occupy the route to Orleans with 300 gentlemen, and to put myself at Your Highness' orders.

DOWAGER

But aren't you afraid that so large a force will awaken suspicions?

LA ROCHEFOUCAULD

Your Highness, these gentlemen are supposed to attend the internment of the Duke de La Rochefoucauld.

PRINCESS

But, Duke, don't we have an escort to join you?

LA ROCHEFOUCAULD

I will leave everyone at Her Highness' disposition.

PRINCESS

Thanks, Duke.

USHER

A gentleman arriving from Guyenne asks to speak to M. Lenet instantly. It's an affair of the greatest importance.

LENET

I am going.

PRINCESS

Not at all—receive him here. It is perhaps essential that the Duke know what you are to say to this gentleman from Guyenne. Come, Duke; and you, Lenet—

LENET

Rest assured, Madame, I understood.

(La Rochefoucauld goes off with the ladies. The Princess soon returns listening to Lenet and Cauvignac.)

CAUVIGNAC

(entering)

Ah, Monsieur Lenet. Your very humble servant, M. Lenet.

LENET

You asked to speak to me, sir?

CAUVIGNAC

Yes, sir.

LENET

Sir, I am waiting for you to have the kindness to tell me on whose behalf you come.

CAUVIGNAC

I come on your behalf, sir.

(He gives him a letter.)

LENET

My letter to Mademoiselle de Lartigues.

CAUVIGNAC

Is this letter really from you, sir?

LENET

Exactly, but this letter had an object.

CAUVIGNAC

Yes—so you could obtain a blank commission from the Duke d'Épernon. Here is the blank commission.

PRINCESS

Oh, three times, thanks, sir. Thanks for my husband. Thanks for my son. Thanks for me.

CAUVIGNAC

This lady is?

LENET

The Princess, sir.

CAUVIGNAC

Your Highness.

LENET

Sir, such a document is too precious for you to abandon it to us without conditions. Only this blank order is really yours, right?

CAUVIGNAC

It belongs to the possessor as you can see—it has no other name than that of Monsieur d'Épernon.

LENET

Did you have an understanding with Monsieur d'Épernon to limit?

CAUVIGNAC

There is no other engagement with the Duke.

LENET

Now, sir, my letter to Mademoiselle de Lartigues said we could make conditions with the bearer of the blank orders.

CAUVIGNAC

Well, here I am, sir, let's deal!

LENET

What do you wish?

CAUVIGNAC

Two things.

LENET

Which are?

CAUVIGNAC

Money, first of all.

LENET

We don't have much.

CAUVIGNAC

I will be reasonable.

LENET

And the second?

CAUVIGNAC

A post in the Princes' army.

LENET

But the Princes don't have any army.

CAUVIGNAC

They are going to have one.

LENET

A post in the army will put you in contact with inferiors and superiors—you couldn't understand. What do you say to a 1000 pounds added to the sum we give you and a commission to raise a company.

CAUVIGNAC

I was going to propose that arrangement to you.

LENET

There remains the money.

CAUVIGNAC

Yes, there remains the money.

LENET

What sum do you wish?

CAUVIGNAC

Fifteen thousand pounds—I told you I would be reasonable.

LENET

Fifteen thousand pounds?

CAUVIGNAC

Or ten thousand and a rank, the five thousand pounds being destined to arm and equip my company.

LENET

We prefer 15,000 pounds and a commission.

CAUVIGNAC

So you agree?

LENET

The deal is done—come sir, I am going to seal your commission and count you your money.

PRINCESS

Lenet.

CAUVIGNAC

(bowing)

Madame Princess.

LENET

You will excuse me?

CAUVIGNAC

Certainly, Monsieur Lenet—go right ahead!

LENET

Wait for me in this room. I will rejoin you.

PRINCESS

Lenet, what are you going to do with this blank order?

LENET

Don't you understand, Madame? I will address the order to the governor of the Fort of Vayres, I will send it to Richon—he introduces the 300 gentlemen he's raised, and once inside, well he shuts the doors—as for the rest—it's up to him.

PRINCESS

Fine! And us?

(to the Dowager who returns with Mme. de Tourville)

Come, Madame, come—it's about our approaching departure.

LENET

In precisely ten hours, we will leave the Château by the little gate in the park. An hour after our departure we will leave our escort who will join us on the way; tomorrow we will join up with the 300 gentlemen of Monsieur de la Rochefoucauld, our forces will be enlarged by all the discontented, and we will arrive at Bordeaux with an army.

DOWAGER

But if they disturb us on the way, Lenet, what will we do? The troops of Monsieur de Saint Aignon are on the road and it's impossible not to encounter some of them—

MME DE TOURVILLE

That's a matter of strategy, and I charge myself with directing our march in such a way that—

PRINCESS

And besides, if we must fight, we fight. The spirit of Monsieur de Condé will march with us and we will conquer.

LENET

In the name of heaven, Madame, listen to an old servant—leave Chantilly as persecuted women not as men in revolt! Our plan is made, don't let it fail. We are sure of a fine escort, with which we will avoid the insults of the road for today, twenty different parties hold the country side and prey indifferently on friend or foe. Ten o'clock strikes. Consent, all is ready.

THE VICOMTESS

(entering excitedly)

Princess! Princess!

PRINCESS

What's the matter, my God. How pale you are!

THE VICOMTESS

What's wrong, Madame, is that a gentleman has just arrived from Chantilly and asks to speak to you on behalf of the Queen.

PRINCESS

Great God! We are lost!

LENET

Not at all. On the contrary, we are saved.

PRINCESS

But this messenger from the Queen is only an observer, a spy perhaps?

LENET

Your Highness is right.

PRINCESS

Then his mission is to keep us in sight?

LENET

What difference if it is not you that he watches?

PRINCESS

I do not understand.

LENET

(to Vicomtess, pointing to the bed)

Do you understand, Madame?

THE VICOMTESS

Oh! Yes! Oh, Madame, I am going to be able to render you a real service.

PRINCESS

What? Dear Vicomtess, you consent?

THE VICOMTESS

Leave, Madame! Leave without delay, leave without noise, the accident whose reality is believed will give me a pretext for receiving the gentleman in bed—we will only let a single light burn—so long as he doesn't have the honor of knowing Your Highness personally—time will be gained for your flight.

PRINCESS

And you will rejoin us?

THE VICOMTESS

As soon as I am free.

LENET

(to Usher)

The princess will receive this gentleman as soon as he presents himself.

USHER

He is down below, at the door of the gallery.

LENET

(to Usher)

Go, fetch him.

PRINCESS

But don't forget the Duke d'Épernon's blank order—it's precious!

LENET

I'll attend to that! If Madame the Vicomtess gives us only half an hour, that's all we need.

THE VICOMTESS

Rest assured—go! go!

(As the Princess escapes, Madame de Cambes lies in the bed, Lenet blows out the candles with one exception. Lenet leaves. The usher enters with Canolles.)

USHER

Who shall I announce to Her Highness, sir?

CANOLLES

Announce the Baron de Canolles on behalf of Her Majesty, the Queen Regent.

USHER

The Baron de Canolles.

THE VICOMTESS

The Baron de Canolles. Oh, my God!

(She draws the curtains. The usher exits.)

CANOLLES

(approaching)

Madame, I have the honor to demand on behalf of Her Majesty
the Queen Regent, an audience with Your Highness. Your
Highness deigns to accord me one. Will Your Highness, now
complete her bounties, by a word, by a sign, that she has indeed
noticed my presence and is ready to listen to me?

THE VICOMTESS

Speak sir, and I am listening.

CANOLLES

Her Majesty the Queen sends me to you, Madame, to assure
Your Highness of her desire that you continue to have good
friendly relations with her.

THE VICOMTESS

Sir, don't speak any more of the good friendship which reigns
between Her Majesty and the House of Condé. There are proofs
to the contrary in the cells of the dungeon of Vincennes. But,
what exactly do you wish, sir?

CANOLLES

I wish nothing Madame, it's the Queen who wishes and not I.

I would be in despair that Your Highness judges me, by the mission I am fulfilling. Day before yesterday, I arrived at Nantes bearing a message to the Queen—the post script recommended the messenger to Her Highness, the Queen ordered me to remain near her and yesterday called me to send me here. I was forced to obey, Madame, but while accepting as was my duty, this mission Her Majesty charged me with, I will dare to say I did not solicit it, and I would have refused it if royalty could be refused.

THE VICOMTESS

But still, what does the Queen want?

CANOLLES

She intends that I live in this Château and that, unworthy as I am of this honor, that I remain here as companion to Your Highness.

THE VICOMTESS

Meaning, be frank, sir, meaning that the Queen wants to spy on us, right?

CANOLLES

If the Queen wants to spy on Your Highness, I am then a spy? I thank Your Highness for her frankness.

THE VICOMTESS

Sir!

CANOLLES

Not at all. I accept the word—treat me Madame as you would treat such wretches. Forget that I am only an atom obeying the breath of a queen, have your lackey chase me out, have your gentlemen kill me, just put me face to face with people to whom I can reply with stick or sword, but do not so cruelly insult a gentleman who is fulfilling his duty as subject and soldier. You, Madame, who are so highly placed by birth, merit, and misfortune!

THE VICOMTESS

Oh—excuse me, sir, pardon me—may it please God that I have no intention to insult as brave an officer as you! No, Monsieur de Canolles, I do not suspect your loyalty. I withdraw my words, they are wounding, I agree. No, no, you are a noble heart, Baron—I do you full and complete justice.

CANOLLES

(aside)

Oh—but I am not mistaken. That voice—I've already heard—that voice is not the voice of Madame de Condé—that voice.

(He goes to the candle.)

THE VICOMTESS

What are you doing?

CANOLLES

Pardon, Madame. I beg Your Highness not to forget, especially in this circumstance, that I am only the passive instrument of an illustrious will. Madame, I am charged by the King to protect Your Highness—I ought, therefore to be sure that it is indeed Madame de Condé I am protecting. I must confirm your identity. I must claim the honor of seeing your face.

THE VICOMTESS

Oh, but this is an insupportable inquisition, sir! If the King gave you the orders, it's because the King is only a child and doesn't yet know the duty of a gentleman. To force a woman to show her face is the same insult as tearing off a man's mask.

CANOLLES

Madame, I am happily unaware how to persecute a woman and even more, how one offends a Princess. There's a word before which men bow when the word comes from Kings, and Kings when the word comes from destiny—Madame—it must be.

THE VICOMTESS

Sir, you forget that I have twenty-five gentlemen and numerous and armed servants—and that if you push me to the last extreme—

CANOLLES

(going to the window)

Madame, you don't realize that within five hundred paces, hidden in the woods which surround Chantilly, I have 200 cavaliers who I can bring together in a few seconds and that a signal from me will suffice—

THE VICOMTESS

Oh, then, sir, this is not an inquisition, it's an act of violence and this obstinate pursuit.

CANOLLES

Madame, it's Her Highness, Madame de Condé whom I pursue and not you—you are not Madame de Condé.

THE VICOMTESS

What do you mean?

CANOLLES

I mean that it no longer rests with me to return to Paris to admit to the Queen that so as not to displease a woman that I loved—I name no one, Madame, so don't let rage into your eyes—I have violated her orders, I have permitted the flight of her enemy, during the time I just consecrated to you—she is rushing at this time on a good horse between Monsieur de la Rochefoucauld, her champion and Monsieur Lenet, her councilor, with his gentlemen and his captains, with all his household even, on the route to Bordeaux and has nothing to do with what is passing at the moment between the Baron de Canolles and the Vicomte or Vicomtess de Cambes! But I can change this scene of mystification into a scene of mourning, as I told you Madame, I have only to open the window—whistle three times with this golden whistle, and in five minutes two hundred cavaliers will have joined and arrested Madame La Princess, garotted her officers who at this time flee and laugh at me, unaware the fools that I have them in my hands.

THE VICOMTESS

Sir, by all things holy, by all sacred principles, sir, don't do that! Don't do that for the honor of the King, for the honor of the Queen, for your honor! Don't do it for your honor! Don't do it— from grace towards me who begs you, for me who honors you, for me who esteems you, for me who loves you.

CANOLLES

(dropping the whistle)

Oh! I am lost.

THE VICOMTESS

What are you saying?

CANOLLES

I say that from the moment I recognized you, I say that from the moment when recognizing you, I let Madame de Condé flee—I say that I am a traitor!

THE VICOMTESS

But what's to be done then?

CANOLLES

Repeat to me that you love me! To each pang of remorse, repeat that magic word that you just said and I will forget everything! Everything! yes, for you render me mad with joy.

THE VICOMTESS

(in his arms)

Well, yes, yes, I love you!

CANOLLES

Oh, Monsieur de Mazarin is rich enough to lose all he possesses, but I am not rich enough to lose the only treasure I possess.

CAUVIGNAC

(entering)

Baron Canolles, in the name of the King, I arrest you.

CANOLLES

Sir!

CAUVIGNAC

Your word!

CANOLLES

The order?

CAUVIGNAC

Here it is!

CANOLLES

You see, Madame, the illusion didn't last long! With the day, the great hunter of phantoms, all my dreams have disappeared. Here is my sword, sir. But I know you it seems to me.

CAUVIGNAC

By God—so you recognize me! It is I who at Jaulnay brought you the order on the Port of the Duke d'Épernon—commission to leave for the court and I've just received this order for your arrest. Ah, sir, your fortune was in this commission—you failed in it—so much the worse for you. Come sir, we are leaving.

CANOLLES

Can I ask you, sir, where you are ordered to take me, and if you are forbidden to give me this satisfaction to know where I am going.

CAUVIGNAC

No, sir, I can tell you. We are escorting you to the fortress island of St. Georges.

THE VICOMTESS

To the Isle Saint Georges?

CANOLLES

Goodbye, Madame, goodbye.

THE VICOMTESS

And I, where are they taking me? For if the Baron is guilty, I am indeed more guilty.

CAUVIGNAC

You, Madame! You can withdraw—you are free.

THE VICOMTESS

Free? Then I can watch over him.

(She leaves by one door—Canolles by the other.)

CAUVIGNAC

Lieutenant Barrabas—you will conduct the prisoner to Fort St. Georges. You will answer for him with your head!

BARRABAS

Then we're on the King's side?

CAUVIGNAC

By God!

CURTAIN

ACT III

SCENE 6

The interior of the Fort of Saint Georges. In the rear a gallery. To the right, the apartment of the Governor.

BARRABAS

Well, sir, the route was long, but now we have arrived.

CANOLLES

It appears they treat me as a man of some importance.

BARRABAS

Yes, my word, the whole garrison is on alert.

CANOLLES

Do you believe I'll remain a prisoner for a long period, sir?

BARRABAS

I don't know, Baron, but from the manner in which you were recommended to me, I should say "yes".

CANOLLES

Do you think they'll question me?

BARRABAS

That's the usual procedure.

CANOLLES

And if I don't answer?

BARRABAS

The Devil—in that case, you know—

CANOLLES

No, I don't know.

BARRABAS

Damn—then there's—then there's the question.

CANOLLES

Ah! Ah! Ordinary?

BARRABAS

Ordinary and extraordinary. It depends on what you are accused of sir.

CANOLLES

I am very afraid of being accused of a crime against the state.

BARRABAS

In that case, you will receive the extraordinary question: ten pots.

CANOLLES

What do you mean ten pots?

BARRABAS

Yes, you will have ten kettles.

CANOLLES

Is water in style in the Isle of St. Georges?

BARRABAS

You understand sir, on the river Garonne—

CANOLLES

Precisely—one has it at hand. And how many gallons are ten kettles?

BARRABAS

Three gallons, three gallons and a half.

CANOLLES

Oh! Oh! I'll never be able to contend with all that.

BARRABAS

But, if you take care to get in with the jailer.

CANOLLES

With the jailer?

BARRABAS

Yes, you will have a good end.

CANOLLES

What, if you please, can the jailer do for me?

BARRABAS

He can make you drink some oil.

CANOLLES

Oil is a remedy?

BARRABAS

Sovereign, sir.

CANOLLES

You think so?

BARRABAS

I speak from experience; I've drunk.

CANOLLES

What—you have drunk?

BARRABAS

I meant to say I've seen drunk.

CANOLLES

Fine!

BARRABAS

Yes, sir, I've seen a smaller man than you drink 10 kettles with extreme ease, thanks to the oil which prepared the way. It's true that he swelled up, as is customary, but with a good fire, they reduced the swelling without too much damage. That's the essential of the second part of the operation—remember these words well—warm without boiling.

CANOLLES

I understand. The gentleman was the executor of important works, perhaps?

BARRABAS

No, sir, no—I never had that honor.

CANOLLES

Assistant then?

BARRABAS

No sir, curious amateur only.

CANOLLES

And your name is, sir?

BARRABAS

Barrabas!

CANOLLES

Fine name, old name—well spoken of in scripture.

BARRABAS

In the passion, yes, sir.

CANOLLES

That's the same thing, but from habit, I said scripture.

BARRABAS

The gentleman is a Huguenot.

CANOLLES

Very Huguenot—there have been many living and buried in my family.

BARRABAS

I hope such a fate is not reserved for you.

CANOLLES

No, they will content themselves with drowning me. But they are very late it seems to me.

BARRABAS

Don't get impatient, sir, for I see an officer who seems to me indeed to have business with you.

CANOLLES

The governor of the place, doubtless he's coming to meet his new tenant.

BARRABAS

In fact, it appears you won't languish like certain persons who they leave for a whole week in the vestibule. You will be locked up right away.

CANOLLES

So much the better!

OFFICER

(entering)

Sir, is it to the Baron de Canolles, Captain with whom I have the honor to speak?

CANOLLES

Sir, I am truly confused by your politeness, yes, I am Baron de Canolles. Now, treat me with the courtesy of one officer towards another, and lodge me the best you can.

OFFICER

Sir, the dwelling is very special, but to anticipate your desires, there are all possible alternatives.

CANOLLES

And to whom do I owe thanks that these anticipations were instituted?

OFFICER

The King, sir, who ordered all this be done.

CANOLLES

Doubtless, sir, doubtless; God protect me from slandering His Majesty especially under these circumstances! Yet, I wouldn't be annoyed to obtain certain information.

OFFICER

I am at your disposal sir, but I will take the liberty to make you aware that the garrison is waiting for you.

CANOLLES

To do what, sir?

OFFICER

To recognize you.

CANOLLES

(aside)

Plague, an entire garrison to recognize a prisoner. Thee are fine manners it seems to me.

(aloud)

Sir, I am at your orders and quite ready to follow you wherever you escort me.

BARRABAS

I think you will be put to the ordinary question.

CANOLLES

So much the better! I'll swell up only half as much.

OFFICER

But first of all, permit me to give you the keys of the fortress.

CANOLLES

The keys?

OFFICER

We are conducting the usual ceremony, according to the most rigorous rules of etiquette.

CANOLLES

Then who do you take me for?

OFFICER

For who you are, it seems to me—for Baron de Canolles.

CANOLLES

And then?

OFFICER

Governor of the Fort of the Isle of Saint Georges.

CANOLLES

Governor of the Fort of the Isle of St. Georges?

(to Barrabas)

No, right?

(Barrabas gives a negative sign.)

OFFICER

In a moment, I shall have the honor to turn over to the Governor the provisions I've received and which notified me that you would arrive today.

CANOLLES

So, I am governor of the Fort and the Isle of St. Georges.

OFFICER

Yes, sir, and His Majesty has made us happy by such a claim.

CANOLLES

You are sure there's no error?

OFFICER

Perfectly sure. Besides the commission and the letter are with me.

CANOLLES

Signed?

OFFICER

Doubtless.

CANOLLES

And I can have this commission, read this letter?

OFFICER

Right now.

CANOLLES

Well, sir, do me the services of finding them, I beg you.

OFFICER

Why, of course! I am going, sir.

(He leaves.)

BARRABAS

Well—Governor?

CANOLLES

Can you explain to me how this came to pass? I admit I have trouble not to take all that has happened to me for a dream.

BARRABAS

My word, sir, the dream is agreeable, especially much more agreeable as you did not expect it. As for me, I admit that when I spoke to you of 10 kettles, my word, I thought was gilding the pill for you.

CANOLLES

You were then convinced—?

BARRABAS

That I bought you here to be tortured, yes, sir.

CANOLLES

Thanks! Now have you arrived at some opinion on what has happened to me?

BARRABAS

Eh! Oh! Perhaps!

CANOLLES

Be so gracious as to expose it to me.

BARRABAS

Sir, here it is. The Queen must have understood how difficult was the mission she gave you. Her first moment of rage passed, she repented and as from all appearances you are not a man to hate, Her Gracious Majesty wished to reward you for having punished you too much.

CANOLLES

Inadmissable, Monsieur Barrabas.

BARRABAS

Inadmissable?

CANOLLES

Unlikely, at least.

BARRABAS

Unlikely?

CANOLLES

Yes.

BARRABAS

In that case, sir, it remains only for me to present to you my very humble congratulations. You can be as happy as a King on the Isle of St. Georges. Good wine, good hunting, fresh fish and the women, sir, the women in the neighborhood of Bordeaux. Ah—that is what's miraculous—

CANOLLES

Very fine.

BARRABAS

(starting to leave)

I have the honor sir—

CANOLLES

Wait—

(He fumbles in his pockets.)

BARRABAS

No use, sir.

CANOLLES

What do you mean, no use?

BARRABAS

Yes, sir, you won't find it.

CANOLLES

In fact, my purse has vanished. But who the devil took my purse?

BARRABAS

I, sir.

CANOLLES

You? And why did you do that?

BARRABAS

So that you could not corrupt me.

CANOLLES

Ah! Ah! Indeed, that's well thought out! Then you took my money?

BARRABAS

And I did the right thing, sir, for if you had corrupted me, which is possible, you would have fled and if you had fled, you would quite naturally have lost the high position which has come to you, and I would be inconsolable.

CANOLLES

Truly, Monsieur Barrabas, you astonish me, and I regret not having a second purse—but wait, I want to see if I am truly the governor of the Isle of St. Georges.

BARRABAS

How?

CANOLLES

I wish to give you a good twenty pistoles from the treasury.

BARRABAS

Useless, sir.

CANOLLES

What? You refuse my twenty pistoles?

BARRABAS

God save me from it! I have never had, thanks to heaven, such false pride.

CANOLLES

Good.

BARRABAS

But I notice, sticking out from a box placed on this table certain strings which I believe are purse strings.

CANOLLES

Your foresight could be very correct, Monsieur Barrabas, for you appear to be familiar with purse strings.

BARRABAS

Indeed so, sir.

CANOLLES

(reading a little paper attached to a purse)

In fact, "a thousand pistoles for the private fund of the Governor of St. Georges."

BARRABAS

Take my compliments, sir—the Queen does things well; unfortunately, she's twenty years older than in Buckingham's times.

OFFICER

(returning)

Here's your commission, sir, here's your letter.

CANOLLES

In fact, there can be no doubt—and now that I am governor of the Fort St. Georges, I am forced to recognize myself as such—when you wish I will stand the review..

OFFICER

At your leave, sir.

CANOLLES

My dear Monsieur Barrabas, I don't run you off, but—

BARRABAS

Yes, but you prefer I should go? That suits me marvelously—and when you have given me—

CANOLLES

Ah, that's true—pardon, dear sir—so, you are leaving us?

BARRABAS

Yes, sir, I am recommended to Monsieur Richon.

CANOLLES

In what capacity?

BARRABAS

As first officer of the garrison of Vayes.

CANOLLES

So, you are serving the King?

BARRABAS

I believe "yes."

CANOLLES

What—you are not sure?

BARRABAS

One is sure of nothing in this world. For example, you promised me 20 pistoles and now—

CANOLLES

That's very true! Here they are—go, go, my dear Barrabas and may God escort you.

BARRABAS

Sir, I am very grateful to you. You have nothing to say to Monsieur Richon?

CANOLLES

A thousand good words—but we are neighbors and we will have occasion to see each other.

BARRABAS

Sir—

(Barrabas exits.)

OFFICER

Sir, I thought that having accomplished the duty of a soldier you won't be annoyed to accomplish the duty of a gallant man.

CANOLLES

The duty of a gallant man? Speak, sir.

OFFICER

You don't suspect what I wish to say?

CANOLLES

No, the Devil take me!

OFFICER

You know someone arrived here this morning?

CANOLLES

Someone?

OFFICER

Someone whose room is there.

CANOLLES

Whose room is there?

OFFICER

And as I presume you would be pleased to see this someone again.

CANOLLES

(stopping him)

Pardon, sir, I am extremely fatigued having travelled night and day—I don't have a clear head this morning—explain to me then, I beg you.

NANON

(appearing)

What! You haven't guessed?

CANOLLES

Nanon!

NANON

Bad brother, who needs must see his sister to remember her—

(to Officer)

Thanks, sir, for having obtained these few moments for me; as you said, Monsieur de Canolles will take the review tomorrow morning.

(The officer leaves.)

CANOLLES

Nanon! Nanon! Nanon! You?

NANON

Yes, me!

CANOLLES

Ah, I understand—it's you who saved me, while I was losing myself like a fool; you watch over me! you are my guardian angel!

NANON

Don't call me your angel, my friend for I am only a demon. Only I, come at a good time, admit it?

CANOLLES

You are right—and this time especially it was just in time, Nanon—you saved me from the scaffold.

NANON

Really? Well, I think so too, if one must speak frankly to you. But how did you—you so clairvoyant, so clever, let yourself be deceived by the prude of a princess?

CANOLLES

My word, I don't know. I don't understand it myself.

NANON

It's because they are tricky, my dear Canolles! Ah, gentlemen, you wish to make war on women! What did they tell me? In the place of the Princess they made you see a woman of honor, a chambermaid, a chump.

CANOLLES

I thought to see the Princess, I didn't know her.

NANON

And who was it then?

CANOLLES

But, as you said, a woman of honor, a chambermaid—how should I know?

NANON

And it's the fault of this traitorous Mazarin, what the devil! When one charges someone with a mission as difficult as this one gives him a portrait.

(Canolles sits down)

If you had had a portrait of the Princess, or even found one in the Château, you would indeed have recognized that it was not she you were guarding. Happily, I followed you, I had previously made Duke d'Épernon sign over the government of St. Georges' to my brother—for you know you are my brother, my poor Canolles?

CANOLLES

I figured it out from reading your letter.

NANON

Eh! Yes! We were betrayed by another brother that I have and who unfortunately is indeed my brother. The Duke was furious—I told him a fine story as you see—which he believed, poor Monsieur d'Épernon. He's got too great a reputation as a diplomat not to be a little naive with the result that you are protected by the most legitimate of unions.

CANOLLES

And you came to wait for me here?

NANON

Yes, you understand: These brave Gascons do me the honor of detesting me, they want to stone me, burn me, I don't know what. I have chosen to retreat to Fort St. Georges to my protector Canolles. Only you in the world love me a little, right my friend? Look, tell me then that you love me and not like a sister.

CANOLLES

Oh, indeed, I would be a real ingrate if I didn't love you after this.

NANON

Well, I have chosen Fort St. Georges to put my gold, my jewels and my person in safety. All is in your hands, dear friend, my wealth and my existence. Will you watch over it all carefully? Tell me, are you a sure friend, faithful guardian?

CANOLLES

(rising)

Well, yes, Nanon, yes! Your possessions and your person are secure near me—and I will die, I swear to you, to save you from the least danger.

NANON

(rising)

Thanks my noble cavalier—oh, I was indeed sure of your generosity and your courage—alas, I wish to be as sure of your love.

CANOLLES

Oh—be certain.

NANON

My friend, love is not proven by oaths. It's proven by actions. I will judge your love from what you do, Canolles.

CANOLLES

(embracing her)

Well, you will judge.

(Drums and trumpets.)

NANON

(aside)

Now he must forget and he will forget.

CANOLLES

What is it?

NANON

Isn't it some honor that the garrison is preparing to render you?

CANOLLES

No, no, these are for news from outside which have come to us. Under arrest for more than fifteen days, I don't know what has happened.

NANON

Oh—I'll put you up to speed briefly. Monsieur Richon with a blank order signed by Monsieur d'Épernon is in possession of the Fort of Vayres—towards which the royal army is diverting itself at the moment.

CANOLLES

I suspected that Richon was for the Princess—but how did this blank order fall in his hands?

NANON

Alas, I am much afraid, my dear Canolles, that it is still another trick of my true brother. He learned, I don't know how, of the need they had at Chantilly for a blank order and exchanged it for my letter—you know the famous letter in which I invited you to supper. He extorted this blank order from Monsieur d'Épernon which he must have given to Madame de Condé.

CANOLLES

But where is Madame de Condé?

NANON

In Bordeaux, where she was received enthusiastically.

CANOLLES

So that we find ourselves six leagues from her?

NANON

Yes.

CANOLLES

And so, from one moment to the next, we could be attacked by the army of the Princess?

NANON

Yes.

CANOLLES

Good! That's all I wanted to know.

OFFICER

(entering)

Pardon, Governor.

CANOLLES

Ah, it's you, sir—what's wrong?

OFFICER

A member of parliament is at the gate.

(A man with a white flag.)

CANOLLES

A member of parliament? And on whose behalf?

OFFICER

On behalf of the Princess.

CANOLLES

Coming from where?

OFFICER

From Bordeaux.

CANOLLES

Ah! Ah! War is seriously declared, it appears.

OFFICER

The army of Bordeaux is not a league from here—you can see it from the parade ground, and if you refuse the propositions that the envoy is charged to put to you, you will be attacked tonight.

CANOLLES

Is this envoy accompanied?

OFFICER

By two guards of the bourgeois militia from Bordeaux.

CANOLLES

Describe the envoy.

OFFICER

A young man, so far as one can tell.

CANOLLES

What do you mean, so far as one can tell?

OFFICER

Yes, he wears a large felt hat and is enveloped in a great cape, so
that I have trouble seeing him.

CANOLLES

And he's waiting.

OFFICER

In the arms room.

CANOLLES

That's well, sir—one moment! Your word, dear Nanon?

NANON

An envoy? What's it mean?

CANOLLES

It means that the Bordelois want to fright me or corrupt me.

NANON

And you are going to receive him?

CANOLLES

I can't spare myself that.

NANON

Oh! My God!

CANOLLES

What?

NANON

I am afraid! Didn't you say that this envoy has come to frighten you or seduce you?

CANOLLES

Are you afraid he will frighten me?

NANON

No, but perhaps he will seduce you.

CANOLLES

Oh, you doubt me to that degree?

NANON

Friend, a grace!

CANOLLES

What is it?

NANON

Permit me to be present at this interview.

CANOLLES

An envoy won't say one word in front of you.

NANON

Hidden.

CANOLLES

Where?

NANON

Behind these curtains. Let me remain near you, Canolles, I have faith in my star—I will bring you luck.

CANOLLES

But if this envoy comes to confide some state secret in me?

NANON

Can't you confide a state secret to someone who has confided her life and fortune to you?

CANOLLES

(smiling and escorting her)

Well, since you absolutely wish it—introduce this envoy, sir.

(The officer leaves.)

NANON

Be blessed for the good you do me!

CANOLLES

Yes, but not a single word which will betray your presence.

NANON

I swear it.

CANOLLES

Go!

(Nanon hides.)

OFFICER

(entering and announcing)

The envoy from the Princess.

CANOLLES

Bring him in.

(The officer leaves.)

THE VICOMTESS

(as a man)

It is I, sir, do you recognize me?

CANOLLES

You, Madame! Oh! What are you doing here?

NANON

(aside)

Ah!

THE VICOMTESS

Sir, I come to ask you, if after the two weeks we've been parted—do you still remember me?

CANOLLES

Oh! Silence, silence, Madame!

THE VICOMTESS

Aren't we alone here?

CANOLLES

Indeed, but someone might hear us through these walls.

THE VICOMTESS

I think the walls of Fort St. Georges are thicker and deafer than that.

CANOLLES

Well—you have a purpose in coming here?

THE VICOMTESS

After what happened between us at Chantilly, sir, I thought you would easily go over to the Princess' party.

CANOLLES

Alas, what could have been then, may no longer be today.

THE VICOMTESS

And why is that?

CANOLLES

Because, since that time, many unexpected events have occurred, many bonds that I thought broken have been renewed! Instead of the punishment that I thought I deserved for having allowed the Princess to escape, the Queen has substituted a reward of which I am unworthy. Today I am bound to the party of Her Majesty by gratitude.

NANON

(aside)

Alas!

THE VICOMTESS

Say by ambition, sir, and I can understand that; you are noble, of high birth, they've made you, at your age, a lieutenant colonel, governor of a fortified installation, that's fine, I know it—but it is not the natural reward of your merit and Cardinal Mazarin is not the only one who appreciates your visit.

CANOLLES

Not a word more, I beg you!

THE VICOMTESS

You forget, sir, that it is not the Vicomtess de Cambes who speaks to you, but the envoy of the Princess. I am charged with a mission to you—I must accomplish this mission.

CANOLLES

Speak. But why exactly did the Princess choose you?

THE VICOMTESS

Sir, it wasn't the Princess who chose me, but I who put myself forward. The feeling you showed me first at Janluay then later at Chantilly made me believe that I was the most agreeable envoy they could send you.

CANOLLES

Thanks Vicomtess.

THE VICOMTESS

Here then is what I propose to you in the name of the Princess— you understand clearly—in the name of the Princess, not mine.

CANOLLES

I am listening.

THE VICOMTESS

You will surrender the Isle of St. Georges on one of the three conditions I am offering you.

CANOLLES

Speak.

THE VICOMTESS

A sum of 300,000 pounds—

CANOLLES

To go any further would offend me, Madame. I have been charged by the Queen with the defense of Fort St. Georges—and I will not surrender it for gold or money.

THE VICOMTESS

Listen to my second proposition.

CANOLLES

To what good? Haven't I repeated to you that I am unshakable in my resolve? Don't tempt me further—it would be useless.

THE VICOMTESS

Pardon sir, but I must continue my offers—aren't you left in complete liberty to refuse them?

CANOLLES

Go ahead, but truly, you are very cruel!

THE VICOMTESS

You will give your resignation, you will retire from the service and in a year, you will accept under the Prince, the grade of brigadier—which commission will be signed for you in advance.

CANOLLES

Thanks that this idea does not come from you. Thanks even more for the embarrassment with which you broach that proposition, not that my conscience would revolt against serving this or that party—no, I have no conviction—who has in this war, except those with a stake in it? When the sword is drawn from its scabbard, let the blow come from this side or that—what does it matter to me! Independent, without ambition, I accept nothing, neither from one side nor the other—I am merely an officer, that's all—but don't forget, Madame, a defector is always a traitor. The first name is sweeter, but the two are equivalent.

THE VICOMTESS

Well, sir, listen to my last proposition, if the order had not been prescribed to me, I would have begun with this, for I knew you would refuse the first two—the material advantages are not things to tempt a heart like yours and I am happy to have foreseen that. For you one must appeal to noble instincts and noble rewards—something besides hopes of ambition and fortune. Listen then.

CANOLLES

Have pity on me.

THE VICOMTESS

If in place of vile self-interest, they offered you something pure and honorable—if they paid for your resignation, then you could resign blamelessly because hostilities are not yet started. This resignation is neither a defection nor a perfidy—pure and simple it is a choice—if, as I say, they paid this resignation with an alliance? If a woman whom you said you love, whom you swore to love, forever—if this woman came, in her turn to say to you "Monsieur de Canolles", I am free, I am rich, I love you, become my husband—let's leave together, to go where you wish, away from all these civil dissensions, away from France". This time, won't you accept?

CANOLLES

Oh! My God! My God!

THE VICOMTESS

But in the name of heaven, sir, answer me. For truly, I can make nothing of your silence. Am I mistaken? Aren't you Monsieur de Canolles? Aren't you the same man who told me in Janluay that you loved me? who repeated it to me at Chantilly? Speak, speak in the name of heaven! Answer! Answer me!

NANON

(falling in a faint)

Ah! I am dying—I am dying!

THE VICOMTESS

A woman.

CANOLLES

Nanon!

(going to Nanon)

THE VICOMTESS

(falling into a chair)

Sir, I understand now what you call duty—gratitude.

(rising)

I understand why you are inaccessible to all these seductions—and I leave you completely to these sentiments, to this duty—to this gratitude. Goodbye, sir, goodbye!

(returning)

Monsieur de Canolles!

CANOLLES

Go, Madame, go.

THE VICOMTESS

Oh! He doesn't love me—and I wretch that I am—oh, I love him! I love him!

(She leaves.)

CANOLLES

Ah! My God! My God! I think that what I am suffering at this moment is worse than death!

CURTAIN

ACT IV
SCENE 7

A room in Nanon's house in Libourne. To the right a table. To the left furniture.

CASTORIN

(mouth full, served by Francinette)

Oh! My God, yes, Mademoiselle Francinette, it is as I have the honor to tell you—you see in me a victim of duty.

FRANCINETTE

(pouring a drink)

A victim! Poor boy!

CASTORIN

That's the word! Meaning, Mademoiselle, that since the day Monsieur d'Epernons' swagger sticks caught me on the way to Libourne, I've become a symbol of perpetual motion. I am no longer a man, I am a centaur. I get off my horse to find time to saddle another.I no longer lie down except on chairs and I sleep no more than a wink.

(Francinette puts her arm around his neck.)

FRANCINETTE

Well, what's wrong with you? Come on!

CASTORIN

Oh! Don't touch me except with great precaution as if I were made of porcelain. I told you that, since I had the honor to see you, or rather since I've had the regret of not seeing you because it was impossible for me to reach you, I have traveled some five hundred leagues and I assure you it's very hard to endure—five hundred leagues on top of one another. Still, if I had leisure to rest, it would be nothing, but I rest just like a ball that touched a racket and one sends me, the other sends me back.

FRANCINETTE

It's not I who send you back, Monsieur Castorin, do me that justice.

CASTORIN

No, it's my master, "Go lie down, my poor Castorin." "Thanks sir." "Sleep well, good friend." Thanks sir." Five minutes later, "Castorin!" "Sir?" "Let's go to Jaulnay." "Yes, sir." To Jaulnay. "En route to Nantes." "Yes, sir." To Nantes again—he has pity on me—he leaves me in Nantes. I was stiff as a hanged corpse. "I am leaving for Chantilly, Castorin." "Yes, sir." "Rest, Castorin." "Yes, sir." "—and then rejoin me in the morning." Twenty-four leagues in twelve hours. "Yes, sir." I arrive at Chantilly, "Where is monsieur? "He's left." "To go where?" "To go to Fort St. Georges." One hundred forty-eight leagues. Nothing much! I arrive at Fort St. Georges—the fort is taken. "Where is monsieur?" "At Bordeaux." I arrive at Bordeaux.

"It's you, Castorin?" "Yes, sir." "Castorin you are going to leave." "In what direction?" "For Libourne." "Yes, sir." I arrive in Libourne, happily this time, Mademoiselle Nanon isn't here and Mademoiselle Francinette is. I have drunk well, I have eaten well. I am going to sleep. Ha, what's that? It seems to me someone is knocking.

FRANCINETTE

(at the window)

A litter, horses, officers.

NANON

(in the street)

Francinette, open quickly, it's me.

FRANCINETTE

Ah, it's Madame.

CASTORIN

Good.

FRANCINETTE

Stay here, you will give her the letter that you've brought. It will put her in a good mood.

(She takes up everything and leaves at the rear.)

CASTORIN

(alone)

I ask you a bit, since she was en route, if she couldn't march a bit easier and not arrive until tomorrow. I don't know what rage these masters always have of coming and going. It's so good to rest.

(sits down)

Ah!

(He falls asleep.)

NANON

(to Francinette entering)

A letter from Monsieur de Canolles, you say?

FRANCINETTE

Yes, Madame—

NANON

And who brought it?

FRANCINETTE

Castorin.

(Castorin wakes up, rises and gives the letter to Nanon.)

CASTORIN

Here, Madame.

NANON

Ah! Thanks!

FRANCINETTE

(to Nanon)

And it hasn't come by accident, no misfortune has come to you from the taking of Fort St. Georges.

NANON

No, nothing.

FRANCINETTE

It's that when a city is taken by assault they say it happens sometimes—

CASTORIN

(asleep on his feet)

What happens?

NANON

(reading)

"Dear Nanon, prisoner, but free in Bordeaux on my word of honor not to flee and not to correspond with the outside—before giving my word, hurried to write you to assure you of my friendship, which my silence might make you doubt. I leave it to you to defend my honor to the King and the Queen. Your brother, Baron de Canolles." Your brother! There's some providence, I hope, too much prudence, alas—

(to Francinette)

Is Monsieur d'Épernon in Libourne?

FRANCINETTE

Yes, Madame, near the King and the Queen. But he's given the order to be warned of your arrival and I am sure that Cortanvaux has already carried it out, and that the Duke will be here in ten minutes.

NANON

Then, there's no time to lose. Paper, pens and ink.

(Francinette puts all this on the table as well as a bell. To Castorin.)

NANON

One would say you are tired, my poor boy!

(She writes.)

CASTORIN

Yes, Madame, one would say so.

(aside)

Just like my master.

NANON

You are going to sleep—at Bordeaux.

(giving him a letter)

Here! This is for your master.

CASTORIN

(sadly)

Thanks, Madame.

NANON

(giving him a purse)

And this is for you!

CASTORIN

(gaily)

They told me truly that Madame was generous.

NANON

Go, my friend, go! Tell your master that he can count on me and that he won't be a prisoner for very long.

CASTORIN

(aside)

Who cares! After the war, I can ask for a place with the King's courier. I will have my recommendations.

(Castorin leaves.)

NANON

There, now we are alone, miss, the Duke has no suspicion?

FRANCINETTE

Well, yes, Madam! The Duke is more mad than ever. When he learned the Fort of St. Georges was taken, he was like a madman. Then when he received the letter in which you told him, that thanks to the cares of your brother, Monsieur de Canolles, nothing had happened to you, he repeated more than ten times. "Dear Canolles! Brave Canolles! I will make him a general."

NANON

Poor Duke—and you told him what happened to us?

FRANCINETTE

Wait, I am sure it's he I hear on the stairs. This way, this way, sir!

(She leaves after the Duke enters.)

NANON

Oh! Dear Duke, it's you? You have no idea of the impatience with which I was expecting you.

DUKE

And I, too!

NANON

You know all that has taken place? You know that Monsieur de Canolles—?

DUKE

Defended himself like a tiger, like a lion.

NANON

Ah! You know that?

DUKE

Don't I know everything? I even know he never surrendered, but they took him by surprise through a subterranean tunnel of whose existence everyone was totally ignorant.

NANON

Then you don't wish him ill because of his defeat, this poor brother? And the Queen—is she angry with him?

DUKE

Not the least in the world. The fate of armies is uncertain. Paulus was beaten at Cannes, Hannibal at Zama and Pompey at Pharsalia

NANON

Then you won't be opposed to ransoming him or exchanging him?

DUKE

On the contrary, I will press for it with all my strength—and in fact—your brother will be free, Nanon—

NANON

What will you do?

DUKE

Tomorrow.

NANON

Oh! Tomorrow! How has it happened?

DUKE

It's very simple, I just learned that the governor of Vayres—

NANON

Richon?

DUKE

Yes—he's been captured. Well, he'll be exchanged for this brave Canolles.

NANON

Oh! That's a grace from heaven, my dear Duke.

DUKE

You really love your brother?

NANON

More than my life.

DUKE

What a strange thing! You never spoke to me of him before that day I was so stupid as to—

NANON

(interrupting him)

So—Duke—?

DUKE

So, I will send the Governor of Vayres to Madame Condé—who will send Canolles to us—and when our brave commander of the Isle of St. Georges returns to Libourne, well, we will give him a triumph! Who goes there?

CORTANVAUX

The Queen Regent is asking for Milord.

DUKE

Do you know why?

CORTANVAUX

Monsieur Richon, the Governor of Vayers has arrived.

(He bows and exits.)

DUKE

You see, dear Nanon, everything falls out marvelously. I will go to the Queen and bring you the safe-conduct.

NANON

So that my brother can be here—?

DUKE

Tomorrow—! Perhaps tonight if he hastens.

NANON

Oh—don't waste a moment. Tomorrow, this very evening—oh! God watch him!

DUKE

Goodbye, darling—I'll be back.

NANON

Go, Duke, go!

(Exit Duke.)

NANON

(alone)

Yes, let him return! And then I'll tell him everything. I will drag Canolles far from all these terrible dangers which surround him ceaselessly—as if they were mere phantoms! Oh! It's too much to suffer from fear for the one you love! Today the scaffold; tomorrow the ball or the bullet.

CAUVIGNAC

(half opening the door)

Well! Good day, dear little sister!

NANON

You again, sir?

CAUVIGNAC

Again! Oh! That's not a very gracious word. I wish you to take part in the joys which are coming to me—I came up without being announced—Francinette warned me that the Duke was with you—I hid myself. I entered when he left and this is the way you receive me—ah!

NANON

It's that every time I see you, sir, some misfortune comes to me.

CAUVIGNAC

Oh! For goodness sake! Wasn't your last commission performed well? Didn't I arrive in time at Jaulnay, in time at Chantilly?

NANON

Enough!

CAUVIGNAC

You are right—let's talk a little about me!

NANON

Yes—what is this sash? What is this braided hat?

CAUVIGNAC

But these are the insignia of my office. I am governor.

NANON

Governor of what?

CAUVIGNAC

Of a fort.

NANON

You?

CAUVIGNAC

Why not? Indeed they made your make-believe brother

governor of Fort St. Georges—so they can make your real brother governor of Fort de Branne.

NANON

And who made you governor of Fort de Branne?

CAUVIGNAC

The Queen, whom I left, and with whom I am in good.

NANON

Some new treason.

CAUVIGNAC

Oh—for goodness sake!

NANON

Still—why have you come?

CAUVIGNAC

Because you engaged to pay me 200 pistoles if I caught up with Monsieur de Canolles on the road to Paris, and I did so.

NANON

(going to the furniture)

That's true! And here are your 200 pistoles.

CAUVIGNAC

And here's your receipt.

NANON

No need.

CAUVIGNAC

Oh! There must be regularity in keeping accounts, as it is not likely to be the last business we'll do together.

NANON

The last!

CAUVIGNAC

Oh! No, for see here, if you continue to carry on simultaneously this noble brotherhood with Canolles, it will be difficult for you to pass me off.

NANON

I am still counting on that heavily and from tomorrow, when the Queen shall have signed the exchange for Monsieur de Canolles, the governor or Fort St. Georges, in return for M. Richon, the governor of Vayres.

CAUVIGNAC

Ah, you are counting on that exchange?

NANON

Well, am I wrong to?

CAUVIGNAC

Yes, I think so.

NANON

Why?

CAUVIGNAC

Because they will not give M. Richon his freedom—they are going to give him a fair trail and hang him.

CAUVIGNAC

For what reason?

CAUVIGNAC

Because he entered Vayres with a false commission.

NANON

With a false commission? Impossible.

CAUVIGNAC

Don't tell that to me.

NANON

Not to you?

CAUVIGNAC

Doubtless. I was the one who named him governor of Vayres.

NANON

You're mad!

CAUVIGNAC

You recall that blank order?

NANON

The Duke's blank order.

CAUVIGNAC

Yes! The one on which he put his famous mark.

NANON

Well?

CAUVIGNAC

Well, I rid myself of it in favor of Richon—with the result that—

NANON

Ah! My God!

CAUVIGNAC

With the result that, as Monsieur d'Épernon has sworn to hang
the bearer of the order and as Monsieur Richon is the bearer—

just as the little king swore to hang anyone who fired a cannon on the royal army, and as Richon fired the cannon—so, you understand!

NANON

But how could he let himself be taken when he was taking such a great gamble?

CAUVIGNAC

Ah! As to that, it was I again who took it.

NANON

You?

CAUVIGNAC

Yes, and I began to think that I never did anything better in my life.

NANON

You, wretch! But why is that?

CAUVIGNAC

I had introduced three or four men into the place—as bandits, there was nothing to say about them—as honest men—much otherwise it appears—well, it appears they surrendered the place without consulting the governor and—

NANON

And?

CAUVIGNAC

And, my word, I wouldn't care to be inhabiting the skin of this wretched, Richon.

NANON

Francinette! Francinette!

FRANCINETTE

Yes, Madam?

NANON

Run after the Duke—let some one get to him even if he is near the Queen and tell him I am waiting for him, asking for him, calling him.

FRANCINETTE

The Duke has returned and is in conversation below with two people. I will run to warn him.

(She leaves.)

NANON

(to Cauvignac after having opened the door)

Leave! Leave!

CAUVIGNAC

Oh! This time I won't say a word and I even admit that I won't be easy until I'm behind the walls of Branne.

(He leaves.)

FRANCINETTE

(returning)

His Lordship, the Duke.

NANON

Come in, sir, come in quickly.

DUKE

You know what's happened to us?

NANON

Yes, I know something of it; but tell me everything.

DUKE

All is discovered!

NANON

What has been discovered?

DUKE

You recall this anonymous accusation touching your supposed love affair with your brother?

NANON

Well?

DUKE

You recall the blank order which was extorted from me?

NANON

Yes.

DUKE

Well, the accuser is in our hands, my sweet, taken in the net of his blank check—like a fox in a snare.

NANON

Oh! My God! But this man, this man—what have you done?

DUKE

What have we done? You are going to see yourself what we have done.

(noise in the wings opposite the window)

Oh, hold on my word, this is falling out marvelously—let's open this window wide—my word, he's an enemy of the King and we are going to see him hang.

(He opens the window.)

NANON

Hang! What are you saying, sir? Hang the man with the blank order?

DUKE

Yes, and he won't escape. Ah! There's the King who's at the window.

NANON

But, sir, this wretch is not guilty, this unfortunate man—

DUKE

Ah! There—they are bringing Monsieur Richon—he's going to hang high and swiftly from a beam in the Hall. That will teach him to slander women.

NANON

But, sir, this man is a brave officer, you are going to murder an honest man. Ah, sir, give orders, there is still time. Give a sign. Stop this killing! Something tells me that this death will bring us misfortune. In the name of heaven, you who are powerful, you who say you never refuse me anything, grant me the pardon of this man, I ask it on my knees, on my knees.

(A cannon shot can be heard.)

DUKE

It's much too late! Look.

NANON

(going to the window)

Ah!

(She recoils, fainting.)

DUKE

(closing the window and going to Nanon)

Come, come! Be less good, less sensitive, dear Nanon! When there's a civil war, you don't play like children.

NANON

No! No! No!

DUKE

And at Bordeaux, especially at Bordeaux, when they see that they had provoked reprisals, when they see us hang their governor, you will see what they will do.

NANON

Reprisals toward Bordeaux! My God! But you are forgetting there are some of our prisoners at Bordeaux—our prisoners—and that? Ah! Damn you, sir, you who have killed him!

DUKE

Killed! Who?

NANON

Don't you understand, blood thirsty maniac, that at Bordeaux there's a captain, a governor prisoner, a wretch on whom the Bordelias will avenge the murder of this man you have assassinated just now? Don't you understand yet that Monsieur de Canolles is at Bordeaux?

DUKE

Ah, it's true—your brother, this poor Canolles.

NANON

My brother, yes, my brother, my beloved friend. He's lost.

DUKE

Not yet, thank God!

NANON

(in despair)

I tell you that he is lost, sir, and that I am dying.

DUKE

Relax, dear Nanon. I've done wrong, but I'll fix everything.

NANON

How's that?

DUKE

The Queen has some friends in Bordeaux, the Governor of Guyenne has gold in his coffers. All that can be done with power and gold, I will do to save Monsieur de Canolles, your dear brother.

NANON

Ah, if you succeed, how I will love you, sir.

(She throws herself at his feet, he raises her, embraces her and goes to the table.)

DUKE

Watch carefully what I am going to write. In a quarter of an hour, the courier will rush this letter on the way to Bordeaux. This evening the King's attorney, Monsieur Lavie, who is with us will have given his orders to the jailer of Monsieur de Canolles, this evening, your brother will be free.

(rising)

To save Monsieur de Canolles, to save the governor of a royal Château, to save the brother of Nanon—I am offering a million, I authorize murder and arson. Is that what you need? Do you find I've repaired my mistake?

NANON

(reading)

So that Monsieur de Canolles shall be free, the governor, the brother of Nanon? Yes, yes.

DUKE

You are satisfied?

NANON

I bless you! Hey! Someone.

(Cortanvaux appears.)

DUKE

Put on your usual disguise. Ride my best horse to death so that in five hours this letter will be in Monsieur Lavie's hands.

CORTANVAUX

In Bordeaux?

NANON

In Bordeaux! Go, sir, go!

(aside)

My God! If he were to accuse me at this moment of having betrayed him, perhaps later tonight he will love me for having saved him?

(They leave by the rear.)

CURTAIN

ACT IV

SCENE 8

The gardens of the house of Madame de Cambes in Bordeaux. To the right, a flight of stone steps giving on an alley of lime trees.

CANOLLES

(entering—to Ravailly)

Ah, you're here my dear enemy! What the devil brings you to this house?

RAVAILLY

I came to get orders from the Princess.

CANOLLES

The Princess is here now?

RAVAILLY

She lives here.

CANOLLES

Bah! The Princess lives with the Vicomtess de Cambes?

RAVAILLY

Two cannon shots fell this morning on the Hotel de Ville which the alderman had put at the disposition of the Princess. The Vicomtess learned of it and came to offer her house, and the Princess accepted.

CANOLLES

Ah! Really—but you seem to be taking your departure.

RAVAILLY

Yes, I am leading a relief party to Monsieur Richon who it appears is very sorely pressed in the Fort of Vayres.

CANOLLES

Then, I won't detain you; Richon is one of my friends—and one of the very best even.

RAVAILLY

What! And you are serving against each other?

CANOLLES

Alas! You know, one of the misfortunes of civil war is not having the right to choose your enemies. But you waste time, my good Richon is calling you—go, sir, go!

RAVAILLY

And you, sir, aren't you thinking of your ransom?

CANOLLES

My word, no! I am doing wonderfully here—I am quite aware
the Queen would exchange me for a high ranking officer or
buy me back with several sacks of gold—I am not worth the
expense. I will wait until Her Majesty has taken Bordeaux. She
will have me for nothing.

RAVAILLY

Well, what are you going to do here?

CANOLLES

What I have done up to now. Women are engrossed by the
war—as for me, I stay by the door of churches and offer holy
water to the devotees.

RAVAILLY

Then, I will tell Monsieur Richon that you are indeed not in
despair to be a prisoner.

CANOLLES

Tell him I have never been so happy.

(Ravailly leaves.)

THE VICOMTESS

(entering)

Take care, Baron, if some day you complain of your captivity, I will repeat what I just heard—

CANOLLES

And I will repeat to you what I've just said—Alas! Yes, I've never been so happy!

THE VICOMTESS

Baron, there's an "alas" which, permit me to tell you, seems to me much out of place in such a phrase.

CANOLLES

No, Madame, on the contrary, it pervades all my thoughts. I am happy when I see you.

THE VICOMTESS

But you didn't see me just now?

CANOLLES

I felt your presence. Do you think one only sees with the eyes of the body? No, when you come near me, I feel a sweetening in the air, flowers becoming more beautiful—I say to myself "She's there." I turn about and I see you.

THE VICOMTESS

You were in such despair when you got here!

CANOLLES

(escorting the Vicomtess and sitting with her)

What do you want—my life was taking a strange turn. Yes, I was desolate—for I let myself be surprised at night—my reputation as a soldier was lost.

THE VICOMTESS

Could you have known of this secret vault, this passageway built under the river which opened in the very heart of the Fortress—a passage known to only a few people.

CANOLLES

I couldn't have known it, but I should have discovered it. Yes, I was desolate, but I saw you once more, this power you have over me, you who conquered from the beginning—whose power has only grown since—you took over. There I again became your slave, and I admit it to my shame, I am happy.

THE VICOMTESS

Are you speaking the truth?

CANOLLES

Do I know how to lie?

THE VICOMTESS

If you don't know how to lie, Baron, tell me then, frankly, honestly, what place does that woman have in your heart, she who was shut up with you at Fort St. Georges, who listened to us, and who fainted when she recognized me for a woman?

CANOLLES

The place she has the right to reclaim a devoted friendship.

This woman loved me before I knew you. I won't tell you what I felt for her, except that it was a love equal to her love—no, poor fearful slave, she didn't insist that one love her. She only asked to be permitted to love. Not thinking how great this love was, profound, real, disinterested. I gave to mine the shape of a caprice—that's all. Even before knowing you, I was an ingrate to poor Nanon! And I tell you, I would truly be the happiest of men—

THE VICOMTESS

If—

CANOLLES

If I had no more remorse.

THE VICOMTESS

Remorse! Remorse!

CANOLLES

Yes, Madame, remorse! For as truly as I am speaking to you, I tell you that I love you, that I love only you. From the moment I told you this there's a woman who weeps, who trembles, who would give her life for me, and who ought to tell herself that I am a coward or a traitor.

THE VICOMTESS

Oh, sir.

CANOLLES

Eh! Madame, didn't I take an oath to defend her? To protect

her? Didn't I answer for her life and liberty?

THE VICOMTESS

Well, you know that she escaped with her life, you know she is free, you know she has rejoined Monsieur d'Épernon.

CANOLLES

Yes, you told me that already.

THE VICOMTESS

Ah, sir, you still love Mademoiselle de Lartigues?

CANOLLES

Madame, if I told you I felt no more for her than a friendly gratitude, I would be lying. Believe me, Claire, take me with this feeling—I am giving you all that I can give of love, and I am giving you much.

THE VICOMTESS

Alas, I cannot accept, for perhaps you are testing a heart more generous than loving.

CANOLLES

Listen! I would die to spare you a tear, and I made her _weep without being moved; poor woman, she has enemies! Those who do not know her, curse her, and those who know her, scorn her. You have only friends—those who don't know you, respect you, and those who know you, love you. Judge the difference between these two feelings—one of which is dictated by my conscience, the other by my heart.

THE VICOMTESS

Thanks, my friend. But perhaps, you are being carried away by my presence and you may repent of it—weigh my words carefully. I give you until tomorrow to reply—if you wish to say something to Mademoiselle de Lartigues, if you wish to write to her or send her a message—even if you wish to rejoin her—you are free, Canolles. I will take you by the hand. I will even lead you outside the gates of Bordeaux.

CANOLLES

It is useless to wait till tomorrow, Madame, I tell you with a burning heart—but a cold head—I love you! I only love you, and I will never love anyone except you.

THE VICOMTESS

Oh! Thanks! Thanks! Well, I believe your word, I believe your oath, I especially believe my own heart—and from this evening—if you want a priest—in the Carmelite Chapel.

CANOLLES

(falling to his knees)

Oh, Madame—how happy you make me!

THE VICOMTESS

Listen, my friend—I need permission from the Princess. Oh! Don't worry—it's simple fortunately—return this evening. Until this evening! Your wife will be waiting for you.

CANOLLES

Madame, all my love, all my life!

THE VICOMTESS

Go, go, Baron! Here's the Princess. We aren't leaving each other, since I am going to busy myself with uniting us forever.

CANOLLES

She's not alone.

THE VICOMTESS

It's Monsieur de la Rochefoucauld.

CANOLLES

Well, what's the matter?

THE VICOMTESS

I don't know, my friend. The sight of this callous man, cold as marble, hard as steel—the sight of this man who always says ill of a friend to please us—the sight of this man makes me ill. It seems to me, I don't know why, it seems to me that the presence of this man will be fatal to us.

CANOLLES

And why's that, Madam? We don't know him and he doesn't know us.

THE VICOMTESS

You are right.

(Canolles leaves.)

LA ROCHEFOUCAULD

(entering)

Yes, Madame, I answer to you for Richon, as much as before, let's agree, as much as a man can answer for another man.

PRINCESS

Since you answer, Duke that's all that's necessary.

LA ROCHEFOUCAULD

Let's understand each other. Madame, I cannot answer for anyone. I gave him to you; you took him—and I believe him to be a very honest man—why, a very honest man—as if I believe in honest people.

PRINCESS

Truly, Duke, you are giving way to despair. And our Bordelais—do you think they will hold out?

LA ROCHEFOUCAULD

Oh! Yes! So long as they see it in their interest. While waiting, Princess leave it to me—I know what we need to promise them.

PRINCESS

That's well, go Duke—I notice a friend of mine there, who not being able to see me at all times during the day has requested an audience with me, which makes me think she has something very solemn to tell me. Go make your promises. I am going to try to fulfill my obligations.

LA ROCHEFOUCAULD

I have the honor to present my respectful homage to Your Highness.

(bowing)

(to Vicomtess)

Madame.

(He leaves.)

PRINCESS

Well, little one—what's so important? You see instead of waiting for you, I've rushed to you!

THE VICOMTESS

Madame, it's that in the midst of the happiness so much due Your Highness, I came to beg you to cast your glance over your faithful servant who also needs a little happiness.

PRINCESS

With great pleasure, my good Claire, and the happiness God may send you will never equal the happiness I wish you! What boon do you wish? Say, and if it is in my power, count in advance, that it is granted you.

THE VICOMTESS

Widow, free, too free! For this liberty weighs more heavily on me than slavery would. I wish to change my solitude for a better condition.

PRINCESS

Meaning you want to get married, right little one?

THE VICOMTESS

I think so, yes.

PRINCESS

Well, so be it! We'll look after that. Oh—rest assured we will have care of your pride. You must have a Duke and peer, Vicomtess. I will find one for you among my followers.

THE VICOMTESS

Oh, Your Highness, takes too much care, and I wasn't expecting to give her such trouble.

PRINCESS

But you are speaking to me as if your choice was already made, as if you had in your hand the husband you ask of me.

THE VICOMTESS

In effect—it's as Your Highness says.

PRINCESS

Truly! And who is this happy mortal. Speak! Fear nothing. Do I know him?

THE VICOMTESS

Your Highness has seen him at least.

PRINCESS

There's no need to ask if he's young!

THE VICOMTESS

Thirty.

PRINCESS

And noble?

THE VICOMTESS

He's a fine gentleman.

PRINCESS

And courageous!

THE VICOMTESS

His reputation is made.

PRINCESS

And rich!

THE VICOMTESS

I am.

PRINCESS

Marvelous! Now, I only need to know one thing.

THE VICOMTESS

Which is?

PRINCESS

The name of the fortunate gentleman who already possesses the heart, and who will soon possess the person of the most beautiful warrior in my army?

THE VICOMTESS

Madame, it's—

(Ravailly, covered with dust enters.)

RAVAILLY

Her Highness! Where is Her Highness?

PRINCESS

Who's that?

RAVAILLY

Ah! Madam!

PRINCESS

Didn't you leave yet, Monsieur de Ravailly?

RAVAILLY

I was already en route, Madame, with five hundred men I was leading to Richon when I learned—I ask pardon of Your Highness for being the messenger of such bad news! When I learned the Fort of Vayres had capitulated—

PRINCESS

The Fort of Vayres has capitulated? Richon surrendered?

RAVAILLY

Alas! Madame, there's no doubt of it.

PRINCESS

Oh—the coward!

LENET

Madame, Richon is not a coward! I answer for him body for body—and if he capitulated, it was because he couldn't do otherwise.

PRINCESS

Eh! Sir, he ought to die rather than surrender.

LENET

Eh, Madame, can one die when one wishes? But at least he's a prisoner with a guarantee, I hope.

RAVAILLY

Without guarantee, sir, I am afraid. They told me it was a major, a lieutenant, who had negotiated, so indeed there may have been some treason involved, and that instead of making conditions, Richon was betrayed.

LENET

Yes, betrayed, sold out! That's it! I know Richon—I know he's incapable of such cowardice, of such weakness. Oh, Madame, betrayed, sold out! Do you understand? Let's busy ourselves with him, right away! Write quickly, Madame, write, I beg you.

PRINCESS

What shall I write, and to whom?

LENET

Why to save him, Madame.

PRINCESS

Bah! My dear Lenet, when one surrenders a fortress, one takes his precautions.

LENET

But don't you understand that he didn't surrender it? Don't you understand what the captain said, "Betrayed, sold out!" That the negotiations were with a lieutenant and not with him? Oh, Madame, I beg you, write to Monsieur de la Mallerad, send a messenger, an envoy.

PRINCESS

And what mission shall we give this messenger?

LENET

That of preventing the death of a brave captain perhaps, for if you do not listen. Oh, I know the Queen, Madame, and perhaps your messenger will arrive too late.

PRINCESS

Too late? Haven't we some hostages? Haven't we at Chantilly, at Montreal, even here—haven't we some of the King's officers or the King's prisoners?

THE VICOMTESS

Oh, Madame, don't do what Monsieur Lenet asks. Reprisals won't gain Monsieur Richon's freedom.

LENET

It's not a question of his liberty—it's a question of his life.

PRINCESS

Well, what they will do, will be done—prison for prison, scaffold-for-scaffold.

THE VICOMTESS

(on her knees)

Oh, Madame, Monsieur Richon is one of my friends—I just asked you for a boon and you promised to grant me it—well,

Madame, in the name of my deep respect, in the name of my unalterable devotion to you, I demand you save Monsieur Richon.

PRINCESS

Well, so be it—give me pen, ink and paper.

THE VICOMTESS

Here, Madame, here's what Your Highness asks for.

PRINCESS

Thanks little one. Find me a messenger.

RAVAILLY

The messenger is already found—here I am. I have only seen Monsieur Richon once or twice but it's been enough to convince me he was a brave and loyal officer.

LENET

(to Vicomtess aside)

Madame, I know not whether you have an interest in some prisoner, but, if you do, believe a man who is your servant in all things—advice should be given to this prisoner.

THE VICOMTESS

Advice?

LENET

Advice not to remain a prisoner if it's possible.

THE VICOMTESS

Yes, you are right. But where will I find him again? And I gave him a rendezvous here—thanks Monsieur Lenet, thanks. I recommend Richon to you.

LENET

Oh—rest assured.

(The Vicomtess leaves.)

PRINCESS

Here, Monsieur de Ravailly—here's a letter for Monsieur de Meilleraie—I hope that enemies though we are he won't refuse it.

(noise in the court)

What's that?

SHOUTS

(outside)

Branne! Branne! The governor of Branne, a prisoner.

LENET

Ah, ah, the governor of Branne, a prisoner! I am not sorry. If the news is true, this will give us a hostage who will answer for

Richon.

PRINCESS

Haven't we the governor of the Isle of St. Georges—Monsieur de Canolles?

MME DE TOURVILLE

I am happy the plan I proposed for taking Branne indeed succeeded.

LENET

Oh, Madame, let's not delude ourselves with a complete victory—chance plays with the plans of men and sometimes even the plans of women.

SHOUTS

(outside)

Death! Death to the Governor of Branne! Death!

PRINCESS

Ah, ah, decidedly it appears there's a prisoner?

LENET

Yes, Madame, and even this prisoner runs the danger of death. Do you hear those threats?

(He runs to the parapet.)

SHOUTS

Death to the prisoner! Death to the governor of Branne. Death! Death!

LENET

(on the parapet)

Hold firm, gentleman, hold firm, Monsieur de Ravailly—take some men and hurry! Courage! courage! Ah—there he is.

CAUVIGNAC

(entering brought in by Ravailly and soldiers)

My word thanks gentleman, for you prevented me from being devoured by those cannibals. Plague—if they eat men like this, the day the royal army assaults your town they will devour it raw.

CROWD

(at the door, in the rear)

Come on, he's a brave fellow. Long live the governor of Branne.

CAUVIGNAC

My word yes—long live the Governor of Branne—I much prefer him to live.

LENET

Monsieur Cauvignac.

PRINCESS

Monsieur Cauvignac in the royal army! Monsieur Cauvignac, governor of Branne. But this smells of high treason.

CAUVIGNAC

Huh! What did Your Highness say? I thought she pronounced the word treason.

PRINCESS

Yes, sir, treason! For under what title do you present yourself before me?

CAUVIGNAC

Under the title of the Governor of Branne.

PRINCESS

Who signed your orders?

CAUVIGNAC

Cardinal Mazarin.

PRINCESS

And how can you serve in the royal army after having taken an engagement in ours?

CAUVIGNAC

But because Her Highness, failing in her engagements to me, discharged me from mine.

PRINCESS

What's the man talking about?

CAUVIGNAC

The truth. I call upon Monsieur Lenet.

PRINCESS

What do you think of this Monsieur Lenet?

LENET

I am forced to admit that it is the exact truth, Madame. Before Your Highness' departure, I had time to give 10,000 pounds to the gentlemen but I lacked the time to give him a commission.

PRINCESS

Still, you recognize yourself my prisoner, right?

CAUVIGNAC

Madame, I'm accustomed to admit the evidence, and I admit too that I much prefer to be the prisoner of a great Princess like you than to be that of the populace which was going to chop me to pieces if M. Lenet hadn't come to my rescue.

(meanwhile La Rochefoucauld has spoken low to the Princess)

Oh! Oh! Who's this fellow?

LA ROCHEFOUCAULD

Would you ask the prisoner if he can give you some details on the death of Monsieur Richon?

PRINCESS

On the death of Monsieur Richon.

LENET

Richon is dead?

CAUVIGNAC

(aside)

The Devil! This is getting muddled!

LA ROCHEFOUCAULD

Yes, and they saw to it his death was degrading.

ALL

Degrading?

LA ROCHEFOUCAULD

Yes.

PRINCESS

What! Richon?

LA ROCHEFOUCAULD

He died the death of thieves and murderers. Richon was hanged.

CAUVIGNAC

(aside)

Ah!

PRINCESS

Oh! But I hope we shall avenge ourselves on that cruelly.

CAUVIGNAC

(aside)

Beware of reprisals!

PRINCESS

Let's go back inside, Duke, we will meet in council. While waiting, take command of the city—I leave to you the care of avenging my honor and your feelings—for before entering my service, Richon was in yours. I had him from you, and you gave him rather as one of your friends than as one of your servants.

LA ROCHEFOUCAULD

Rest assured, Madame, I will remember what I owe myself and you over this poor dead man. Let the Governor of Branne be escorted to the Château Trompette, Monsieur de Ravailly, don't go away—there will be some orders to execute while waiting, guard the exits. Come, Madame.

CAUVIGNAC

(aside)

This is going bad! This is going bad! This is going bad!

(The clock strikes ten.)

(Cauvignac, the Princess, and La Rochefoucauld exit with followers. Ravailly posts sentinels.}

CANOLLES

(appears at the rear)

Ten o'clock—that's really it. Come on, my heart is more at ease, I have written this poor Nanon to tell her everything is finished between us—then—strange things as if I were pursued by some unknown danger. I went into a church and prayed. Claire didn't tell me if I ought to ask for her.. Let's wait.

RAVAILLY

That's it, sergeant. Two men at the foot of the stairs. Two men at this door.

CANOLLES

Oh! Oh! Who's speaking there?

RAVAILLY

It seems to me I see someone. Have orders already been given me?

CANOLLES

Ah! It's your Monsieur de Ravailly?

RAVAILLY

(aside)

Monsieur de Canolles—poor fellow!

CANOLLES

Haven't you left yet on your expedition?

RAVAILLY

On the contrary, I've already returned.

CANOLLES

Ah!

RAVAILLY

(aside, seeing Lenet enter)

Monsieur Lenet!

LENET

(aside)

That officer.

CANOLLES

What did you just say?

RAVAILLY

(a low voice)

I, sir? I was saying that, if I were a prisoner of war, on parole, for fear that parole wouldn't be kept with me, I would jump on a good horse, I would reach the river, I would give 10 crowns, 20 crowns, 100 crowns to a boatman and my word the next day—whatever happens, happens.

CANOLLES

Ah! You were saying that?

RAVAILLY

Yes, sir.

CANOLLES

And to whom were you saying that, Captain?

RAVAILLY

To myself, since I would risk my commission if I said it to anyone else.

(going off)

My word, I did what I could.

CANOLLES

(to himself)

What do these words signify?

LENET

Monsieur de Canolles.

CANOLLES

Monsieur Lenet?

LENET

Do you know the news?

CANOLLES

No, but tell me, I want to know.

LENET

I haven't the time, but rush over to the cloister of the Carmelites and you will find Mme de Cambes who will tell you.

CANOLLES

Madame de Cambes? But she told me to wait for her here.

LENET

She's changed her mind. Go without losing a moment, and if she isn't there—wait for her in the darkest corner, till she comes to rejoin you. Do you have money?

CANOLLES

What for?

LENET

You never know—in times of civil war—you may need to leave a spot at the moment you least expected it.

CANOLLES

(aside)

Oh! Oh! Both of them are telling me the same thing in different ways.

LENET

You hesitate.

CANOLLES

No, sir, I am going.

(He separates.)

LENET

(seeing Ravailly receive an order)

I believe it was in time.

THE VICOMTESS

(entering)

Ah, it's you.

CANOLLES

Yes.

THE VICOMTESS

What are you doing here?

CANOLLES

I was waiting for you.

THE VICOMTESS

Well, I am searching for you.

CANOLLES

Well?

THE VICOMTESS

Come!

CANOLLES

Where?

THE VICOMTESS

Come, I tell you!

CANOLLES

But—

LENET

Go or it will be too late.

CANOLLES

I am following you.

SENTINEL

You cannot pass.

THE VICOMTESS

What! I cannot pass?

SENTINEL

You, yes, but the not the gentleman.

LENET

Try the other.

SECOND SENTINEL

No one can pass!

THE VICOMTESS

Oh!

CANOLLES

Ah! I understand the advice they gave me.

RAVAILLY

My dear colonel, I am in despair from new measures taken by the council of the Princess.

CANOLLES

You are arresting me? Oh, speak frankly. I've been accustomed to being arrested for some time that if I pass a week without being under arrest, it will astonish me.

RAVAILLY

You won't be deprived except for a short time of your liberty. I hope—

CANOLLES

But I was already a prisoner?

RAVAILLY

Only you had the city for your prison, whereas now—

CANOLLES

That's right—now you escort me to the fortress?

RAVAILLY

It's not my fault, Colonel—I already said enough, it seems to me, and at least to add that Monsieur Richon was dead.

CANOLLES

Thanks, Monsieur Ravailly—thanks, Monsieur Lenet.

Madame—I commend myself to your prayers.

THE VICOMTESS

Oh, my God! What to do?

LENET

The order comes from the Princess, she can revoke the order she has given—leave Monsieur de Canolles and occupy yourself with the Princess.

THE VICOMTESS

Baron, fear nothing—I am here, I watch. Tomorrow, oh, tomorrow I swear to you, you will be free.

CANOLLES

Try to be the one who announces my freedom to me, Madame, it will be a double joy to me.

RAVAILLY

Are you ready, Monsieur de Canolles?

CANOLLES

I follow you, gentlemen!

(exit Canolles, Ravailly, and guards.)

THE VICOMTESS

(to Lenet)

Madame is there?

LENET

Yes, but with Monsieur de la Rochefoucauld.

THE VICOMTESS

Great God! I must speak to her instantly, without delay.

LENET

Let me inform her. But I think it's useless.

(La Rochefoucauld, Madame de Tourville, officers enter.)

MME DE TOURVILLE

Ah, it's you Monsieur Lenet! My word, it was fortunate you weren't present.

LENET

And why, Madam?

MME DE TOURVILLE

Because for the first time my plan prevailed.

LENET

Ah! You are for reprisals, I take it.

MME DE TOURVILLE

Yes, as everyone else—unanimous for reprisals.

THE VICOMTESS

Pardon, Madame, I am less familiar than you with the terms of war—what do you mean by reprisals?

MME DE TOURVILLE

I mean that what has been done to Monsieur Richon will be done to the first royal officer we have in our hands.

THE VICOMTESS

Richon has been arrested, put in prison? Richon is dead?

MME DE TOURVILLE

Richon was judged, condemned and executed.

THE VICOMTESS

Richon has been executed!

MME DE TOURVILLE

Richon has been hanged, my dear, and we are looking for an officer of the royal army to hang him.

LA ROCHEFOUCAULD

But it seems to me this officer is already found, and that by order of the Princess, Monsieur de Canolles has already been arrested.

THE VICOMTESS

Monsieur de Canolles.

LA ROCHEFOUCAULD

Yes, or indeed Monsieur de Ravailly must have disobeyed.

THE VICOMTESS

No, no, Monsieur de Canolles has indeed been arrested here in front of me—just now even. But this is a trick isn't it? Duke, a warning that's all. One cannot do anything, it seems to me at least, one can do nothing to a prisoner on parole.

LA ROCHEFOUCAULD

Madame, Richon was a prisoner on parole.

THE VICOMTESS

Sir, I beg you.

LA ROCHEFOUCAULD

Useless, Madame, this is a decision about which there's no going back. An officer of the royal army will be executed as was Monsieur Richon—come gentleman.

(He leaves with officers and Mme de Tourville.)

THE VICOMTESS

(to Princess entering with Lenet)

Oh, Madame, in the name of heaven, hear me, don't repulse me.

PRINCESS

What's wrong, my child, and why are you crying?

THE VICOMTESS

I am crying, Madame, because I've learned that in council you voted for death—and now Madame, you cannot kill Monsieur de Canolles?

PRINCESS

And why's that? They indeed killed Monsieur Richon.

THE VICOMTESS

But, Madame, recall this is the same Monsieur de Canolles who saved Your Highness at Chantilly.

PRINCESS

Ought I to give him credit for being duped by our ruse?

THE VICOMTESS

And there's the error, Madame, it's that Monsieur de Canolles recognized me—he had two hundred men at the Gate of Chantilly that he could call with a whistle—perhaps he was wrong but he sacrificed his duty to his love.

PRINCESS

So he loved you then?

THE VICOMTESS

He loves me. But the one I just now asked you for permission to marry was—it was Monsieur de Canolles, Madam! I made Monsieur de Canolles prisoner at St. Georges since it was I who betrayed this unknown secret passage, so reflect, Madame, if you kill him, it will be I who have brought his death.

PRINCESS

My dear child, think what you are asking is an impossible thing—Richon is dead—Richon must be avenged.

THE VICOMTESS

Oh, wretch, wretch that I am—it is I who have ruined him, the man I love.

LENET

Madame.

PRINCESS

Ah, you too, Lenet?

LENET

Pardon Madame, they said the death of Monsieur Richon must be avenged on an officer of the royal army.

PRINCESS

Well, isn't Monsieur de Canolles an officer of the royal army?

LENET

True, Madame, but this adventurer, this governor of the town of Branne, this Monsieur de Cauvignac, is also an officer the royal army.

PRINCESS

Ah—the gentleman with the severed arm! Meaning you ask the life of the one in exchange for that of the other? Is that just?

LENET

Firs to fall, it is just, Madame, that when a single man must die, that one does not make two die, it is enough to blow out only once this torch lit by the hand of God, and that one calls life. Furthermore, it is just, if a choice must be made, to save an honest man in preference to an intriguer.

PRINCESS

Well, my old, friend, be content! Be happy, my sweet Claire! Reassure yourselves, both of you—only one will die since you wish it. But don't come back to me demanding grace for the one who is destined to die.

THE VICOMTESS

Oh! Thanks, Madam! From this moment my life and his belong to you.

LENET

In doing this, Madame, you will be at once just and merciful, which up till now has been the privilege of God alone.

THE VICOMTESS

And now, Madame, can I see him? Can I free him?

PRINCESS

See him, yes—deliver him, no. But you have my word as Princess, Claire—go bring him to her.

THE VICOMTESS

A word from you, Madame, to enter the fortress?

PRINCESS

(sitting and writing)

Here it is.

(While she is writing, the Vicomtess is on her knees, kissing the hem of her dress.)

LENET

Why are princesses so rarely happy—it's really such an easy thing to do!

PRINCESS

Because they don't often have councilors like you near them, Lenet.

THE VICOMTESS

(taking the pass)

Oh, thanks, Madame, thanks!

CURTAIN

ACT V
SCENE 9

The prison.

RAVAILLY

Monsieur de Canolles! Sir.

CANOLLES

(seated)

Sir?

(turning to Ravailly)

RAVAILLY

Would you like some supper?

CANOLLES

Willingly.

RAVAILLY

In that case give your orders. The jailer is ordered to give you food, that's agreeable.

CANOLLES

Really? Come, it appears I will be treated honorably while I remain here. That's always something.

RAVAILLY

I am waiting!

CANOLLES

Ah, that's true! Excuse me, your question provoked certain thoughts. Let's return to the subject. Yes, my dear friend, I will eat, I'm very hungry, but I am sober, and a soldier's meal will suffice for me.

RAVAILLY

Now, you have no recommendation to make?

CANOLLES

None!

RAVAILLY

In the town?

CANOLLES

In the town? Why in the town?

RAVAILLY

Yes, aren't you waiting for something? Look, you just told me you are a soldier, I am, too—behave towards me as you would with a comrade.

CANOLLES

No, dear friend, I have no recommendation to make in the town, I await nothing. It's true, I am indeed waiting for someone, but I cannot tell you the name—as for your friendly offers, thanks, my dear lieutenant; if I have need of you, I will tell you so frankly.

RAVAILLY

For the moment, all you ask is for supper—

CANOLLES

Well?

RAVAILLY

You are going to be served, sir—goodbye!

(Exit Ravailly.)

CANOLLES

(alone)

What a solemn air he has on the subject of food! Don't people eat in prison? How this dinner all alone, reminds me of the one I had alone at Biscarros Inn the day Richon refused to sit with me. Poor Richon! He was a brave fellow. War is such a stupid thing. Alive yesterday, dead today. It would have been better for him to die on his cannons, the intrepid man! As I would have done at St. Georges, but for that cursed tunnel. Ah, the reversals are irritating—the death of Richon will double the rigors of my captivity—they won't give me the run of the city, no more rendezvous in those beautiful gardens—! Perhaps they will see me cooped up 15 feet underground, rather than be able to live and spread out in the sun near a beloved woman. A poetic wish transformed by a brutal deception! No more of marriage, for Claire won't be satisfied with a prison chapel. Bah—still be content—one is married just as well in one chapel as another.

(noise, shouts outside)

Ah—they're bringing my supper.

(Two soldiers carrying a table. Canolles looks out the window through the bars.)

CANOLLES

What the devil's going on in the town! Where are all those people going? It seems to be the esplanade. There's neither a parade nor an execution at this hour. They're running the same way—again! Well, my place is set.

(he eats)

Some Bordeaux—it will be good for these good men as for me—

(to soldiers)

My friends, drink this bottle to my health, I drink to yours—

(he drinks, the soldiers drink, and pass the bottle)

They are not well mannered but they enjoy the drink—you cannot have everything.

RAVAILLY

(entering)

Sir—excuse me.

CANOLLES

Ah—that me. Have you come to dine with me?

RAVAILLY

I am unable to have that honor, sir, I ate and I came back to—

CANOLLES

To keep me company? It's very kind of you.

RAVAILLY

(giving a sign to the soldiers to leave. They exit)

No, sir, I came to ask you if you are Catholic or Huguenot?

CANOLLES

What an idea! Why's that?

RAVAILLY

Here in the prison, we have only a Catholic chaplain. That will trouble you, if you are of another religion.

CANOLLES

In what would this trouble me?

(rising)

RAVAILLY

(embarrassed)

When saying your prayers.

CANOLLES

Oh rest easy, I won't think of that so late—I only say my prayers in the morning.

RAVAILLY

So be it, sir, so be it.

(He solutes and leaves.)

CANOLLES

More and more solemn. Ah, that's it, but they are mistaken. Since the death of poor Richon, all those I see have the air of idiots or madmen—I would give tomorrow's supper to see a reasonable face.

THE VICOMTESS

(throwing herself on his neck)

Ah!

CANOLLES

Good! Another madman! Ah, why, Claire! You here! Oh, pardon, pardon me for not having recognized you.

THE VICOMTESS

Yet! Yet! Oh, my God—how happy I am, thanks, thanks, my God for having been able to see him again.

CANOLLES

Again? Having seen me again? And you say this weeping. Eh! Why then can't you see me again?

THE VICOMTESS

Oh! Don't laugh, your gaiety makes me ill—! Don't laugh, I beg you! I have had so much trouble to come to you. If you knew to what lengths I went—without Lenet, without this excellent friend who got me the permission to see you for half hour—but let's speak of you, my friend. Is it really you I find—it's indeed you?

CANOLLES

Why yes, it's really me.

THE VICOMTESS

Stop—don't pretend this false joy—it's no good. I know everything—they didn't hide it from me.

CANOLLES

Ah! They didn't hide it from you?

THE VICOMTESS

They didn't know that I love you—

CANOLLES

My dear, I don't understand exactly—

THE VICOMTESS

Admit that you were expecting me, that you were angry because of silence, that you were accusing me already—

CANOLLES

I was waiting for you, tormented, unhappy, but I didn't accuse you of anything—why would I have done that? "Something kept her"—I told myself, "by some circumstance stronger than her will." The greatest misfortune to me is that our marriage will be deferred, put off a week—two perhaps.

THE VICOMTESS

Are you talking seriously?

CANOLLES

Why, yes.

THE VICOMTESS

You weren't more frightened than that?

CANOLLES

Frightened? By what? Did I run some danger without suspecting?

Ah, anything is possible.

THE VICOMTESS

The wretch! He didn't know.

CANOLLES

Ah—oh—something is wrong—no, I didn't know—I still don't know but as I am a man, as I am your friend—you are going to tell me, right, Claire? Look, I beg you, speak.

THE VICOMTESS

You know that Richon is dead?

CANOLLES

Ah, that's it, yes, I know it. Ah, I understand my arrest, my interrogation, I understand the officer's offers of service. The silence of the soldiers, I understand your behavior, your joy at seeing me again, your tears, the shouts of the crowd going to the esplanade. Richon is dead, right—and they are going to avenge Richon's death on me?

THE VICOMTESS

No, no—my beloved, no poor friend of my heart, you will not be sacrificed dear victim! Oh! You were not mistaken. Yes, you were intended to perish, you've been close to death, my handsome fiance. But reassure yourself—we can speak of joy, of a future. I saved your life and I am going to consecrate mine to you—it won't be your blood which will pay for Richon's blood.

CANOLLES

Someone will die, you say? Oh, dear friend, silence! Silence! This is impossible.

THE VICOMTESS

Yes, silence! The other one might hear us—our joy would be a crime.

CANOLLES

Who will die? Who then?

RAVAILLY

(entering)

Madame, the half hour is up.

THE VICOMTESS

Already?

CANOLLES

Already!

THE VICOMTESS

(to Ravailly)

Yes, sir!

(to Canolles)

Look, instead of being so sad, rejoice with me. Tonight, in an hour perhaps you will leave the prison. The pardon has been signed, then without losing a minute, we will flee. This cursed town suffocates me. So laugh then. Goodbye. Oh, not goodbye—till we meet again, till we meet again.

(She exits.)

CANOLLES

Ah, my dear Ravailly.

RAVAILLY

Now, sir, if it's not enough to be happy, you must be compassionate.

CANOLLES

Compassionate?

RAVAILLY

Yes, your neighbor, the other governor, he asks to see you.

CANOLLES

The other governor?

RAVAILLY

The governor who was taken like you—the poor man is going to die.

CANOLLES

He wants to see me?

RAVAILLY

Do you consent to it?

CANOLLES

Do I consent to it? Oh, I think so, indeed, poor unfortunate. I await him, I open my arms to him; I don't know him, but never mind.

RAVAILLY

Oh—he knows you very well.

CANOLLES

Does he know he's been condemned?

RAVAILLY

I don't think so.

CANOLLES

Oh! Let us keep him in ignorance, my God! Go quickly—bring him to me, sir. I beg you, go quickly.

RAVAILLY

I am going. Till we meet again.

CANOLLES

Return with him, and stay with us.

RAVAILLY

No, I return to my post. From eleven o'clock the jailers alone remain in control of all matters in the prison. Yours has been warned—he knows your companion will be in your cell—when the moment arrives he will come to take him—so when you see him come—

CANOLLES

This is horrible!

RAVAILLY

Till we meet again, when you are free.

CANOLLES

Thanks.

(Ravailly exits)

My God—don't let the wretch come to reproach me about my happiness!

CAUVIGNAC

(entering)

Much thanks, officer! It is Monsieur de Canolles who is there?

RAVAILLY

(behind the door)

Yes.

CANOLLES

His voice makes me ill.

CAUVIGNAC

Baron, you allow me!

CANOLLES

Eh! Sir, it's you?

CAUVIGNAC

You recognize me?

CANOLLES

By God! Do I recognize the man who twice caused me so much
trouble—first at Jaulnay—then at Chantilly—I should think I
recognize you!

CAUVIGNAC

You are indeed very good, thanks! Well, what do you think of
this precarious situation—difficult, eh? Haven't you seen from
your cell, as I have seen from mine all these blockheads running
to a certain place which must be the esplanade? You know the
esplanade, my dear fellow, and you know what purpose it is
used for?

CANOLLES

To pass in review, yes.

CAUVIGNAC

(aside)

Come on, another one who doesn't understand his position. He must be prepared a bit—to soften the fall.

(aloud)

Sir, my dear sir, you look on things a little too cheerfully. Reviews, reviews, that's weak—I think it's a question of something more—a little execution, for example.

CANOLLES

Come now!

CAUVIGNAC

Ah, you are reassured? So much the better—you don't have the reasons I have.

CANOLLES

To be afraid!

CAUVIGNAC

To be uneasy! Ah, don't boast too much about your affairs, it's not great looking—go, but if I must say it yours is nothing to mine. And mine is terribly confused. Do you know who I am?

CANOLLES

That's a singular question. You're Captain Cauvignac, governor of—

CAUVIGNAC

Of Branne, yes—for the moment, but I didn't always bear the name Cauvignac; I haven't always been governor of Branne.

CANOLLES

Ah—what did you call yourself, when you didn't call yourself Cauvignac?

CAUVIGNAC

For example, one day when I didn't call myself Cauvignac, I called myself Baron de Canolles, like you.

CANOLLES

Huh?

CAUVIGNAC

Yes, I understand—you are wondering if I am really in my right senses.

CANOLLES

My word, yes—unless you can explain to me—

CAUVIGNAC

Ah, well, a sole word—my real name is Roland de Lartigues—

Nanon is my sister.

CANOLLES

You, the brother of Nanon? You? Ah, poor boy!

CAUVIGNAC

Well yes, poor boy, very poor boy—for besides a host of little disagreements which resulted in a trial that brought me here, I have the disgrace to call myself Roland de Lartigues, and to be Nanon's brother.

CANOLLES

And what has become of Nanon, Monsieur de Lartigues— what's she doing?

CAUVIGNAC

Oh, by god, she weeps—not for me—she unaware of my arrest, but over you—whose fate she knew from the hour it happened.

CANOLLES

Relax, Lenet won't say that you are the brother of Nanon, Monsieur de la Rochefoucauld has no reason to receive you— they don't know anything of all this.

CAUVIGNAC

So be it, but they will know one thing—they will know, for example that it was I who gave to Monsieur Lenet a certain document signed by Monsieur d'Épernon and that this signature caused—bah! Let's forget that, let's forget that.

CANOLLES

Look, Monsieur de Cauvignac—courage!

CAUVIGNAC

Eh, by God, do you think I lack it? You will see me at this famous moment when we make our tour of the esplanade. For me, one thing bothers me—will we be shot, decapitated or hanged?

CANOLLES

What are you talking about? Men of the sword—

CAUVIGNAC

Well, wasn't Richon a man of the sword? That didn't prevent him from being hanged.

CANOLLES

Hanged! Richon! A soldier? Oh, my God!

CAUVIGNAC

You didn't know that? Judge the situation now. Yes, hanged! I was at Libourne when they tried this poor Richon. Well, trial, judgment, execution, lasted all of 10 minutes. We are already behind schedule.

CANOLLES

What's this? They're coming.

CAUVIGNAC

The devil.

CANOLLES

I asked for wine—perhaps the jailer is bringing it.

CAUVIGNAC

Ah! It could still be that. If the jailers come with bottles, it will be all right—but if he comes empty handed.

JAILER

Which if you to is Baron de Canolles?

CANOLLES and CAUVIGNAC

Ah! The Devil!

CANOLLES

I've born that name for 30 years and it is sufficiently known so that I don't hesitate to admit it.

CAUVIGNAC

As for me, I've borne it for 3 hours, that's enough to make me very uneasy.

CANOLLES

I am Monsieur de Canolles.

JAILER

You were governor of some place?

CANOLLES

Yes.

CAUVIGNAC

And I too, not counting that I am called Canolles like this gentleman. Ah, let us explain carefully to each other and without scorn—what happened to Richon is enough without my causing another man's death.

JAILER

(to Canolles)

So, Canolles is the name you bear now?

CANOLLES

Yes.

JAILER

(to Cauvignac)

And you are also sometimes known as Canolles?

CAUVIGNAC

Alas, yes.

JAILER

And you are both governors?

CANOLLES and CAUVIGNAC

Both of us!

JAILER

Happily I have one last question to put to you, and this question will clarify everything.

CAUVIGNAC

Ah! Put your question.

JAILER

Which of you two is the brother of Nanon de Lartigues?

CAUVIGNAC

(to Canolles)

Sir, I told you, that would be what they attack me for.

CANOLLES

Oh!

JAILER

Well?

(The Vicomtess enters.)

CAUVIGNAC

And if I told you I was the brother of Mademoiselle de Lartigues—what would you say to me?

JAILER

I would say—follow me.

CANOLLES

Plague! Thanks.

CANOLLES

Mademoiselle Nanon also calls me her brother.

JAILER

Ah! Try to understand, gentlemen, the thing is worth the trouble. It is a question of life and death.

CANOLLES

All the more reason for me to assert my name—de Canolles.

CAUVIGNAC

And I, sir, my title is the brother of Nanon.

CANOLLES

Still—

THE VICOMTESS

My friend! My friend!

CANOLLES

You—you—you here?

JAILER

Look, hurry up, gentlemen, I need to know what to do.

CAUVIGNAC

What a hurry you are in.

THE VICOMTESS

(to Canolles)

Sir! And I? And my life—and all our future? And this pardon that I have, sir—? Oh, you don't love me then? But you cannot say you are the brother of this woman! Don't lie, sir, don't lie!

CAUVIGNAC

Come, come, I've done enough in my life that others have paid for to pay in my turn today.

CANOLLES

(aside)

The wretch!

THE VICOMTESS

Let me leave—let this man be led off.

JAILER

Come on, let's decide!

CAUVIGNAC

Hola, my friend, softly—dear companion, I am determined on one point—that that's that I go first.

JAILER

Let's go, sir!

CAUVIGNAC

Patience, you, you are tiring my good man. Dear brother— dear brother-in-law, Madame, a thousand compliments—ah Madame, this gentleman will do me the justice to say that it is not I who take you from him.

CANOLLES

Goodbye.

CAUVIGNAC

A word, if you please.

CANOLLES

Speak.

CAUVIGNAC

Pardon, Madame.

(to Canolles)

Do you pray sometimes?

CANOLLES

Yes.

CAUVIGNAC

Well, when you pray, say a Pater and Ave for me.

(to jailer)

It is I who am the brother of Mademoiselle de Lartigues—her true brother—March, my good fellow.

(Exit Cauvignac and the jailer.)

THE VICOMTESS

As for us, let us leave, my friend, let us leave.

CANOLLES

Yes, let us leave.

(officers enter)

What's this?

(La Rochefoucauld, Lenet, officers enter.)

THE VICOMTESS

(to La Rochefoucauld)

Sir, there's the order to release Monsieur de Canolles.

LA ROCHEFOUCAULD

Very well, Madame the gentleman is free.

VICOMTESS

Come my friend.

CANOLLES

We are leaving, gentlemen.

(bowing)

LENET

Go quickly.

LA ROCHEFOUCAULD

Didn't they tell me another person was in this cell with Monsieur Canolles?

OFFICER

Yes, Milord.

LENET

(low to Canolles)

Leave now!

THE VICOMTESS

(to officers hedged about)

Allow us, gentlemen.

LA ROCHEFOUCAULD

Excuse me, Madame.

THE VICOMTESS

What now, Duke?

LA ROCHEFOUCAULD

I don't see the other prisoner.

LENET

They must have taken him to his cell in #3.

THE VICOMTESS

Sir, is there any purpose in my waiting if the Princess has signed the pardon for Monsieur de Canolles?

LA ROCHEFOUCAULD

Yes, certainly not.

THE VICOMTESS

Well, here's the order—do you recognize it?

CANOLLES

You can go, Madame, the Duke will accomplish the formalities.

LENET

(low)

Go! Go!

THE VICOMTESS

Oh, but come, come now!

OFFICER

No. 3 is empty, the prisoner is no longer there.

LA ROCHEFOUCAULD

Ah! Ah! You see! Don't let anyone out, gentlemen!

THE VICOMTESS

Sir—

CANOLLES

(aside)

I understand everything. Nanon was watching over me, Nanon named me as her brother to Monsieur d'Épernon. Nanon, unaware of Cauvignac's arrest freed her brother—I am dead.

THE VICOMTESS

I will pass! I will pass! I tell you! I have the order in the name of this gentleman—I will pass.

LA ROCHEFOUCAULD

Madame, that doesn't matter to me anymore; the Princess pardoned one of the prisoners, but she intends to punish the other—the other one having disappeared.

THE VICOMTESS

Oh!

LENET

Monsieur Duke.

THE VICOMTESS

You would disobey Her Highness!

LA ROCHEFOUCAULD

No, Madame, but I am going to inform her of what has happened—I am going.

LENET

(low to Vicomtess)

Don't let him go.

THE VICOMTESS

(to Lenet)

Oh! No!

(to Duke)

Why you?

LA ROCHEFOUCAULD

It's time, Madame—you then. Who knows the spirit of the Princess better than you?

LENET

(low to Vicomtess)

Don't go!

LA ROCHEFOUCAULD

Well, are you going, Madam?

THE VICOMTESS

I won't leave this gentleman.

OFFICER

(to Canolles)

Monsieur de Canolles—step away.

CANOLLES

(low)

I understand.

(aloud)

Listen, dear Claire, I have great confidence in the Duke, but I admit it, I have much more confidence in you—what the Princess will refuse to another, she won't refuse to the Vicomtess de Cambes.

THE VICOMTESS

Is it you who tell me this?

CANOLLES

It's I who tell you this.

THE VICOMTESS

I am going to her. Lenet! Lenet! Swear you won't leave him.

LENET

I won't leave him. I swear it.

THE VICOMTESS

Thanks! I will return.

CANOLLES

Goodbye!

LENET

Embrace her now!

CANOLLES

(embracing her)

Claire!

THE VICOMTESS

Let me run to the Princess, let me—

(in the back)

I will return! I will return!

(She leaves.)

LA ROCHEFOUCAULD

(to Canolles)

Sir, we are waiting for you.

CANOLLES

Me? But aren't you going to wait for the return of Mme de Cambes?

LA ROCHEFOUCAULD

You are allowed to separate from the woman you love; that is all that can be done for you.

CANOLLES

(to Lenet)

I understand. I won't see her again. When you told me to embrace her—it was for the last time?

RAVAILLY

One would say he weeps!

CANOLLES

Pride alone and real courage come to my aid! I weep over such a futile thing as life. Come on, what did I do at Fort St. Georges when a thousand deaths threatened me? I fought, I laughed.

(guards enter)

Well, today, as on that day, if I cannot fight at least nothing shall prevent me from laughing. Excuse me, gentlemen, I need a minute to accustom myself to death—if it's too much, excuse me gentlemen for making you wait for me. Whenever you wish, I am waiting for you.

(He calls Lenet, takes his arm and leaves with him.)

CURTAIN

ACT V

SCENE 10

The Esplanade—night.

Nanon and Cortanvaux on the contrescarp, the executioner's helper eating at the foot of the gallows. Cauvignac and the jailer leaving by the covered way.

NANON

Nothing yet! My friend, did you really deliver the letter to the King's Attorney himself?

CORTANVAUX

To him personally.

NANON

And he went to the prison right away?

CORTANVAUX

That very instant!

NANON

And he returned—you are saying this to reassure me?

CORTANVAUX

He returned telling me he answered for everything.

NANON

So, Monsieur Canolles, my brother, will be able to flee by the Postern gate?

CORTANVAUX

By the Postern gate.

NANON

On the side of the Esplanade?

CORTANVAUX

On the side of the Esplanade.

NANON

Which is right here, correct?

CORTANVAUX

Here the postern, here's the Esplanade.

NANON

Yes, it's true—and these terrible machines of death.

(The guard on the Esplanade thinks he's heard talking— approaching and looking about.)

CORTANVAUX

Silence, Madame! The guard has heard us—and if he sees us—

SENTINEL

Hey! Down on the other side of the ditch—is somebody there?

(Cortanvaux and Nanon hide and remain mute)

SENTINEL

My mistake.

(The Sentinel continues to patrol.)

CAUVIGNAC

(entering behind the jailer)

Eh! But one moment, friend! Where are you taking me?

JAILER

Come!

CAUVIGNAC

Come! That's well said—but one prefers to know where one is going.

JAILER

Come, I tell you. We are there.

CAUVIGNAC

Where's that?

JAILER

At the Postern gate.

CAUVIGNAC

The Postern gate?

JAILER

One second—

CAUVIGNAC

What are you doing?

JAILER

Extinguishing my lantern.

CAUVIGNAC

We won't be able to see anything.

JAILER

Bah! And the stars?

CAUVIGNAC

What of the stars?

JAILER

(opening the gate)

Yes!

CAUVIGNAC

But what is this! How dark it is! It seems to me to be like
Acheron.

JAILER

These are the moats of the city.

NANON

It seems to me I heard—

CORTANVAUX

The noise of the gate, right?

NANON

Hush.

(She looks over the side.)

CAUVIGNAC

The moats—ah!

JAILER

Do you know how to swim?

CAUVIGNAC

Yes—no—yes—I mean why the devil do you ask me that?

JAILER

Because, if you know how to swim, we won't be forced to wait for the boat which is stationed down there—but that's a quarter of an hour lost, and during that time, they may notice your flight and recapture you.

CAUVIGNAC

Ah, indeed! Why I'm fleeing then. Why then, we are escaping!

JAILER

By God! Of course we are escaping.

CAUVIGNAC

And where to?

JAILER

Where you please.

CAUVIGNAC

Then I'm free?

JAILER

Free as the air.

CAUVIGNAC

Ah!

(He jumps into the water.)

CORTANVAUX

I seem to see two shadows.

NANON

And I, I hear some voices.

CAUVIGNAC

(on the other side)

Ouf! there I am—dear jailer of my heart, God will reward you.

NANON

Is it you my friend?

CAUVIGNAC

Really—there's someone.

NANON

Is it you?

CAUVIGNAC

(low)

The voice of my sister!

(aloud)

Yes, it's me.

NANON

(to Cortanvaux)

Leave the wagons there and go ready the horses.

CORTANVAUX

Yes.

NANON

Oh, my God, I thank you, he is saved.

(recognizing her brother)

Cauvignac!

CAUVIGNAC

You weren't expecting me?

NANON

Wretch! Where is Monsieur de Canolles?

CAUVIGNAC

Why, in prison, I should think.

NANON

No, no, not in prison for there he is. There he is.

(The people come forward pushing back the guards and place themselves so they can see the execution.)

NANON

Oh! Wretch that I am.

CAUVIGNAC

Well, for the first time, I've had any conscience, it must be admitted that the thing has turned out badly enough.

NANON

Canolles! Canolles!

CAUVIGNAC

Wait, perhaps all is not lost!

NANON

Oh!

SENTINEL

Who goes there?

CAUVIGNAC

Silence! Poor boy, it's he who will be hanged!

(Canolles, Lenet, the officer, soldiers and people come in.)

CANOLLES

Oh! I would indeed like to see her yet one more time.

LENET

Do you wish that I go find her? Do you want me to fetch her?

CANOLLES

Oh! Yes! Yes!

LENET

Well, I will rush together; but you will kill her.

CANOLLES

No, stay!

RAVAILLY

(to Canolles)

What are you saying, sir?

CANOLLES

I said that I didn't think it was so far from the prison to the Esplanade.

LENET

Alas, don't complain sir, for you have arrived.

CANOLLES

That's well.

(he takes off his cloak and gives it to a soldier, and he embraces Lenet)

Let's go.

(going up the first step, then turning his head, he shouts)

What's that I see there—? What is that lugubrious and shape-less thing that I can hardly distinguish in the night?

(to soldiers who have climbed up ahead of him)

Light up the way—why, I'm not mistaken, it's the hideous silhouette of a gibbet. But that's not what I have the right to expect—that, gentlemen! It's not a scaffold, it's not an ax, it's the not the block.

(His eyes turn toward Ravailly.)

RAVAILLY

Alas, sir.

CANOLLES

Where is the Duke de La Rochefoucauld? I wish to speak to the Duke de La Rochefoucauld.

LENET

What do you wish to tell him?

CANOLLES

I wish to tell him I am a gentleman, everyone knows it—the executioner himself is not unaware of it—I am a gentleman and as such, I have the right to have my head chopped off.

RAVAILLY

Alas, sir, the King hung Richon. And it's a question of reprisals.

CANOLLES

I don't ask for mercy, I demand justice! Ah—you are not content simply to kill me, you intend my death to be infamous! There are people who love me, gentleman, well, in the heart of these people, you will forever imprint the ignoble memory of my death on a gibbet—ah, not a weapon—

(going to Ravailly)

Sir, you are an officer, you are a gentleman, sir, for mercy, for pity, a blow of the sword, a musket ball, whatever you like so long as it is something that kills! Ah, I don't want to die the death of a criminal, of murderers, of cowards—! I don't want that! I don't want that!

(He reaches the side of the people. Lenet comes near him.)

NANON

(to the jailer)

My friend, my fortune to get me back to the town—escort me.

CAUVIGNAC

What do you want to do?

NANON

They detest me. They hate me, they curse me—I am going to offer myself in his place. To have me, they will let him go.

CAUVIGNAC

Sister! Sister!

CANOLLES

My friend, my friends, a knife, a knife,—throw me a knife—from mercy, for pity.

THE VICOMTESS

(in the distance)

Let me see him at least before he dies.

(Canolles and the Vicomtess throw themselves in each other's arms.)

BOTH

Oh!

NANON

My God, save him, do it for her!

(The executioner approaches and touches Canolles' shoulder.)

CANOLLES

That's all right. I am ready—do your office.

NANON

A look at me! A single look.

CAUVIGNAC

(to Cortanvaux)

Hold that woman.

(taking a carbine behind a tree)

Monsieur de Canolles! Monsieur de Canolles!

CANOLLES

(stopping)

I understand.

(He thrusts his chest forward. Cauvignac fires. Canolles totters and falls, saying)

Thanks! Claire! Claire!

THE VICOMTESS

Oh!

(She hurls herself on his body.)

NANON

Happier than I even to the end.

CURTAIN

ABOUT THE AUTHOR

Frank J. Morlock has written and translated many plays since retiring from the legal profession in 1992. His translations have also appeared on Project Gutenberg, the Alexandre Dumas Père web page, Literature in the Age of Napoléon, Infinite Artistries. com, and Munsey's (formerly Blackmask). In 2006 he received an award from the North American Jules Verne Society for his translations of Verne's plays. He lives and works in México.

www.ingramcontent.com/pod-product-compliance
Lightning Source LLC
Chambersburg PA
CBHW021213090426
42740CB00006B/204